CW00766068

Céline

Stéphane-Joseph Piat, O.F.M.

Céline

Sister Geneviève of the Holy Face

Sister and Witness of Saint Thérèse of the Child Jesus

Translated by
The Carmelite Sisters of the Eucharist
of Colchester, Connecticut

IGNATIUS PRESS SAN FRANCISCO

Title of the French original:
Céline: Sœur Geneviève de la Sainte Face,
Sœur et témoin de Sainte Thérèse de l'Enfant Jésus
Second edition,

Cover photograph:
Céline and Thérèse (1881)
courtesy of the Office Central de Lisieux

Cover design by Roxanne Mei Lum

ISBN 0-89870-602-5
Library of Congress catalogue number 97-70157
Printed in the United States of America ∞

Contents

Foreword

Céline has already taken her place in history alongside that of her sister, Saint Thérèse of the Child Jesus. This biography of Céline, written by Father Piat, will therefore be welcomed by the innumerable devotees of Saint Thérèse of the Child Jesus as a delightful complement to the "autobiographical manuscripts" of the Saint. No one was better suited to write this life than Father Piat, who, by his excellent work *The Story of a Family* has introduced us to the Martin household and acquainted us with the saintly parents of Saint Thérèse of the Child Jesus. More than anyone, he knew each member of the Martin family. Today he presents Céline as the witness of Saint Thérèse of the Child Jesus. The subtitle of this work underlines the most important aspect of Céline's mission and the one that must hold our very special attention.

Four years older than Thérèse, Céline was constantly at her side. "We are like two little chicks", Thérèse told Louise, the maid, "that cannot be separated." And in saying that, they embraced and held each other tightly. At the boarding school, Céline was the big sister and protector of Thérèse, who, grief stricken over the death of her mother, had become shy and tearful. Céline was the first to notice the effects of the wonderful Christmas grace of 1886, which suddenly confirmed the psychological maturity of Thérèse and lit the path of perfection for Thérèse by placing her on the threshold of Carmel, where she would want to enter the following Christmas.

Céline also accompanied Thérèse on the trip to Rome and was her confidante in her plan to speak to the Holy Father despite all the prohibitions. They were two spiritual sisters. The prospect of soon being separated bound them even closer together and prompted the opening of their hearts to each other in the belvedere of Les Buissonnets, proof of their intimacy and their burning desire for the Beloved who had conquered them.

The Christmas grace had changed the nature of their relationship. When she entered Carmel, Thérèse felt like a mother to Céline, who was left behind to be near their father and whom she overwhelmed with affectionate solicitude in the crucifying trial of his illness. Thérèse cherished the dream of having her dear Céline join her in the same Carmel. After M. Martin's death in 1894, the almost insurmountable difficulties that prevented the realization of this dream suddenly fell away, and Céline was again at the side of Thérèse. She was a novice in the novitiate of the Lisieux Carmel, where Saint Thérèse of the Child Jesus had become the assistant novice mistress. This was also the time when in the soul of Thérèse the doctrine of spiritual childhood was worked out in the depths of anguish and darkness.

Céline's entrance into the Lisieux Carmel was providential. Thérèse then dared to explain her teaching in order to give it as the most precious treasure of her soul to the one who became, from this time on, her disciple. In my opinion, this sisterly affection had considerable influence on the inspirations that poured from the soul of Thérèse, who had become a great contemplative and mistress of the spiritual life. Would Thérèse have had the courage to confide to others as she did to her sister the lights that welled up in her anguished soul, and would she have dared to urge them to follow in her little way? It is doubtful. When Thérèse, on June 9, 1895, sought permission to offer herself to Merciful Love, it seemed normal to her to ask the same permission for Céline, who had become Sister Geneviève. She would not have known how else to set out on this path that leads to the consuming furnace of Merciful Love except in the company of the one who was doubly her sister, both by reason of blood ties and, from then on, by even stronger spiritual ties. Thus, Céline became the witness of Thérèse's loftiest spiritual ascents. She was also there at her bedside when the Saint was in her death agony on the afternoon of September 30, 1897. She was witness to a death like that of Jesus on the Cross which Thérèse had so much desired, witness to the sufferings that so alarmed Mother Agnes and Sister Marie of the Sacred Heart. She had the privilege of receiving from Thérèse the last glance before her final ecstasy. She also gathered up the last tear that fell from her eyelids.

Father Piat describes in detail Céline's relationship with her sister; he also describes precisely the transformations of that soul whom Thérèse's death had left full of memories and insights. Céline would always be Thérèse's witness, but from then on in another way. She would use her gift for painting to show us what Thérèse looked like. Would she be perfectly successful? She portrayed her with admirable sincerity, as she saw her and understood her to be. The sincerity of witnesses, above all if they are very fond of their subject, does not always coincide with objectivity.

Be that as it may, when Thérèse, through her canonization, came to belong in a special way to the Church—since her writings like her doctrine would no longer be the exclusive property of her family but would become the property of the Church—Céline had no greater desire than to dispossess herself in order to give up everything, including the manuscripts and personal remembrances of Thérèse. This is how the "autobiographical manuscripts" came to be given to the public in their complete original form.

It would seem that Céline had then accomplished her mission as witness. Not at all. It remained for her to witness by her personal achievements. Her witness here was of the highest value. She wanted to live this doctrine of spiritual childhood that she had received and transmitted. Was not her temperament an insurmountable obstacle for such an enterprise? Although the daughters of M. Martin were born into the same household, enriched by the same Carmelite vocation, and formed in the same spiritual family, each had her own personality marked by very different characteristics. On the day of her jubilee of religious profession, Céline was told that she was as intimately united to Thérèse as John was to Jesus, although she was a "son of thunder" like the beloved disciple. She knew better than anyone just what a daughter of thunder she was and would remain. Such as she was, she had placed herself under the direction of her holy sister and carried out her teaching; the outbursts of her nature nourished her humility and her spiritual poverty. Here, the pen of Father Piat excels in the description of the struggles that these contradictions engendered, of the transformation that, little by little, was worked in her, of the triumph we witness in Céline's last months on earth, which show her to us under the influence of Merciful Love as it took hold of her, worked its final purifications, and at last carried her away.

This last testimony of Céline is no less valuable. Have we not, in commenting on some of Thérèse's expressions, especially that of "little souls" to whom she addresses her doctrine, wrapped her teaching in childish forms that conceal rather than illustrate it? Have we not diminished its scope under the pretext of clarifying it for the souls for whom it was intended? Thérèse's doctrine has a universal scope; she herself stated that she wanted it to be carried out up to the most advanced age and even by those in the highest positions. It was not reserved to certain people only; Céline's example is superabundant proof of this. Her life, written by Father Piat, will be a pressing invitation and an invaluable encouragement to many souls whom a certain kind of "little Thérèse" (if not universally accepted, at least rather widespread) has kept at a distance from the great spiritual mistress of our times.

FATHER MARIE-EUGÈNE DE L'ENFANT JÉSUS, O.C.D.
Notre-Dame de Vie, Christmas, 1962

P.S. In finishing this foreword, I came across an unpublished extract from Céline's personal papers. I cannot resist the pleasure of presenting this delightful fable to our readers, because, written in the style Thérèse was fond of using with Céline, it suggests the happy conclusion of the relationship between Thérèse and Céline.

When I was alone with my Thérèse I said to her: "You want to see a charming little bird like you hatched from a sparrow's egg; it's impossible!"

"Yes, but I will do a trick to amuse all the saints. I will take the little egg and tell the saints: 'Now watch closely, I am going to perform a sleight-of-hand trick: Here is a little sparrow's egg, very well! I am going to make a pretty little bird like me come out of it!'

"Then I will whisper ever so softly to God while presenting my little egg to him: 'Change the nature of the little bird by blowing on it. . . .' Then, when he gives it back to me, I will take it to the Blessed Virgin and ask her to kiss it. . . . After that, I will entrust it to Saint Joseph and beg him to caress it. . . . Finally, I will say in a very loud voice so that all the saints can hear:

" 'Now all of you say that you like the little bird that is going to come out of the little egg as much as I do!'

"Immediately all the saints will cry out: 'We like the little bird that is going to come out of the little egg as much as you do!'

"I will then crack the little egg with a triumphant flourish, and a pretty little bird will come sit beside me on God's lap, and all the saints will be in an indescribably joyful mood while listening to the singing of the two little birds."[1]

[1] August 4, 1897, unpublished memoirs of Sister Geneviève of the Holy Face.

I

Life at Home with Thérèse

I. The First Steps at Alençon

Céline Martin—in religion, Sister Geneviève of the Holy Face—followed in the footsteps of Thérèse as the "sweet echo of my soul". She was at the same time her sister, her disciple, and her witness. Her merit lies in having believed in Merciful Love and in having been the first to follow the "little way". By her life, which was replete with struggles, and by her death, which was genuinely holy, she gave proof of what God does in a soul who, despite—or, better still, because of—its weaknesses delivers itself up to him as a little child. The example is worth remembering.

There is no lack of documents to help us paint her portrait and outline her work. We benefit from the vast amount of research prompted by Thérèse's glory. We have at our disposal, too, a brief autobiography that Sister Geneviève was requested to write in 1909 by the prioress at that time, Mother Marie-Ange of the Infant Jesus. It originally bore the title: "Story of a Brand Snatched from the Fire", for which Mother Agnes of Jesus substituted a less provocative title: "Story of a Little Soul Who Has Passed through a Furnace", since she knew it was on the whole only a matter of struggles and trials in the midst of an innocence that had remained intact.

Marie-Céline Martin was born on the rue du Pont-Neuf in Alençon on April 28, 1869, the seventh of nine children, five of whom survived. She was baptized privately on the day she was born, according to the custom of that time, and the complementary rite of baptism was administered to her on the following September 5. When her mother discovered that she had symptoms of the same illness that had robbed her of two previous baby boys, she became alarmed and placed her for a few months in the care of a nurse.

Even though the little one remained frail, she was endowed with amazing energy. She was passionately attached to her father. They found her "mischievous as a little devil" and already willful. "Again! Again!" she cried when they had her take her first steps. A little street urchin once slapped her in the face, throwing Céline into a fit of anger. However much they appealed to the love of Jesus, she replied: "What does this have to do with Jesus? He is indeed the Master, but I too am mistress." It was only in the quiet of the night that she was led to forgive and to say: "I truly love the poor now."

It is true that their servant Louise, who reproached herself for having given too little attention to Hélène,[1] took Céline under her wing. If Céline's parents had not put a stop to it, she would have spoiled her quickly. In truth, she was, as M. Martin would say later of Thérèse, "a pretty, strapping girl" with her clearly defined features, her unusually lively eyes, and a certain resoluteness in her overall bearing that was, nevertheless, covered with genuine sweetness. Once, in the middle of the street, when she and Louise passed in front of a military post, Céline did not hesitate to call out loudly, as if it were a profession of faith: "I will be a religious."

She was intensely alive, already curious about everything,

[1] Hélène was Thérèse's sister who had died at age five a few years before Thérèse's birth.

multiplying her "Whys?". Later, she herself would discern "in the budding aptitudes of little Céline two tendencies: one was an insatiable need for life and happiness, more than her nature could restrain; the other, a very tender heart." "It was not hard to predict", she modestly concluded, "whether, with such dispositions, balance would be easy to maintain."

Mme Martin was more optimistic. In the letters she sent to her sister-in-law and to Pauline at the boarding school in Mans, she drew this delightful miniature of the child: "What a sweet little thing she is! No one has ever been so attached to me; no matter how much she wants to do something, if I tell her she's bothering me, she stops immediately."

"My little Céline is altogether given to virtue; it is the innermost feeling of her being; she has a candid soul and has a horror of evil. I think this child is going to give me great consolation; she has a noble nature. She displays the best dispositions and is going to be a very pious child. It is truly rare to see such inclinations to piety in one so young."

"She chatters like a magpie, she is charming and witty. . . . She learns anything she sets her mind to; her sisters have only to sing a little song four or five times and Céline can repeat it perfectly, but as soon as she notices they are listening to her, she stops."

"She is very intelligent; she has learned all her letters in two weeks."

"She takes care of her things as children rarely do, and she prefers not to use them rather than risk their being broken."

"It takes her only a short time to learn a catechism lesson by heart or some point of Bible history—and all without much effort on her part."

A headstrong personality already showed through her smile. Witness this reference drawn from the *Conseils et souvenirs* of Sister Geneviève: "I was three or four years of age when I was taken for a walk in the country to a delightful spot dotted with spring flowers. I stopped in front of one of them that was prettier than all the others. But coiled by its elegant stem was a little snake that turned its venomous head toward me. To give up the flower for such a little thing was certainly not in my character, which never knew how to reckon with obstacles, and I was just getting ready to pluck it when a great cry of alarm made me draw back. Someone had noticed me and, picking me up, removed me from the danger."

The birth of Thérèse endowed Céline with an inseparable companion four years her junior. The family now lived on rue Saint-Blaise. Together they played under the arbor and counted their "practices", which quite intrigued their neighbors, who did not know this word referred to acts of virtue; they played with Jenny, the daughter of the prefect who owned the Hotel Louis XIII, which, behind an immense main courtyard, occupied the other side of the street. When Marie, the eldest in the family, gave Céline her first lessons, Thérèse insisted on being present; there were only minor incidents, quickly remedied, such as when Céline reproached her for always having her own way with her dolls.

Their mother again made note of their deep-seated harmony and its rare interruptions: "There is Céline playing a game of building blocks with the little one; they argue from time to time, but Céline gives in in order to have a pearl in her crown."

"They are all they need to amuse each other; every day, as soon as they have eaten, Céline goes to take her little rooster; at once she catches the hen for Thérèse. I can never manage to do that myself, but she is so quick that she has it with the first leap. Then the two of them come in with their animals to sit in a corner by the fireplace and amuse themselves for hours on end."

"We are like two little chicks that cannot be separated", exclaimed Thérèse as she cuddled up against her sister in bed.

"I have never seen two children love each other more", concluded Mme Martin. "When Marie comes to look for Céline for her class, poor little Thérèse is all in tears. Alas! What happens to her when her little playmate goes away."

The Saint herself recalled this close relationship. "I remember that indeed I was not able to remain without Céline. I preferred to leave the table without finishing my dessert rather than not follow her as soon as she got up to leave." Not being able to accompany Céline to Mass, Thérèse would rush to her on her return and ask her for some blessed bread, or, if there were none, beg her to make some herself, with a big sign of the cross.

Education received in such a milieu, where faith governs everything, tends to form strong characters and convictions. Their parents lived only for God, with the sole intention of accomplishing his will. They understood authority to mean service, which consisted in directing the souls confided to them toward the good. By example, more than by words, they instilled virtue and piety, knowing how to correct faults, inspire generosity, and make the most austere lessons attractive. Young children, observers and imitators that they essentially are, cannot be indifferent when they see those whom they cherish most attend daily Mass, observe strictly the abstinences and fasts stipulated by Church law, sanctify Sundays with inviolable fidelity, supernaturalize the duties of their state, venerate priests, take an active part in parish affairs, and preside over the different rituals of the family liturgies: morning and evening prayer, grace before and after meals, Marian devotions during the month of May. Charity was the soul of the household. It was displayed with good humor and blossomed during the evenings, the outings, and the family recreations for which only the cloister could erase the nostalgia.

Sister Geneviève appreciated the magnitude of this gift: "I consider the greatest grace of my life was to have had Christian parents and to have received from them a vigorous education that left no place for petty vanities. In our house, nothing was ever sacrificed to human respect. The only altar erected was that to God alone, and if sometimes the sacrifices seemed austere, the time always came when I enjoyed their delightful perfume."

II. Life at Les Buissonnets

The death of Mme Martin on August 28, 1877, shattered this youthful happiness. "You will be my mamma now", said Céline to Marie, while Thérèse turned to Pauline. In fact, Pauline would be the one who assumed the spiritual motherhood of both of them, while the eldest sister, Marie, took over the running of the house. They moved to Lisieux, into the gracious residence of Les Buissonnets, in order to be near their uncle Guérin. Life resumed, intimate and warm, but a change had taken place in the psychological behavior of the two little girls. "I, who had been so sweet," attests Céline, "became an imp full of mischief, while her high-spiritedness [referring to Thérèse] was instantly cloaked under the appearance of excessive timidity and sensitivity. Except for that, the roles were changed, for she was constantly the image of moral strength, and I was of the greatest weakness."

Their union of heart, however, did not change. It is touching to see Thérèse, at six years of age, testifying to her feelings on little scraps of ruled paper, which, taken together, constitute a candid letter in which each word overflows with inexpressible tenderness:

My dear little Céline,
You know very well how much I love you.
Goodbye, my dear little Céline.
Your little Thérèse who loves you with all her heart.
Thérèse Martin

Céline enrolled as a part-time boarder at the Benedictine Abbey. Although placed with students older than she, she easily advanced to the head of the class and kept that place up to the end. Official reports that have been preserved indicate her application to her studies. If she found it difficult to learn things word for word, her logical and inquisitive temperament spurred her to investigate everything thoroughly. Except in arithmetic, she easily took the first prizes. Not that she pursued academic successes on her own accord; her heart remained at Les Buissonnets. It cost her much in the evening to tear herself away from the family to isolate herself in her room to do her homework. She confessed to having wished at times for some change like a flood or an earthquake in the city, or even a mad dog, because those would have been the only acceptable reasons for staying home—a headache or a toothache was not a valid excuse.

With a mastery that merited the praises of M. Guérin, Pauline prepared Céline for her First Communion. She put together for her, as she later did for Thérèse, a little book where, under the symbol of flowers, the little girl could record her sacrifices and her pious thoughts. She made a very fervent retreat, although the full regime at the boarding school seemed cruel to the little one, despite visits from M. Martin and Thérèse. The ceremony of May 13, 1880, made a deep impression on Céline. She wrote,

It was with an inexpressible joy that I received my Beloved. I had waited a long time for him. Ah! what things I had to say to him! I asked him to have pity on me, to protect me always, and never to permit me to offend him; then, I gave him my heart forever and promised that I would be completely his. . . . I felt sure that he deigned to accept me as his little spouse and that he would fulfill the role of my protector that I had confided to him; and I felt that he had taken me into his safekeeping and would preserve me always from all evil.

I recall that I had to recite the Act of Humility and that I was very happy about it. . . .[2] In the evening, it was I who recited the Act of Consecration to the Blessed Virgin. Oh! how happy I was to say those words in the presence of everyone in order to give myself irrevocably to my Mother in heaven, whom I loved with incomparable tenderness. It seems to me that in accepting for her own the little orphan who knelt at her feet, she adopted her as her own child.

A short time after my First Communion . . . I received the sacrament of confirmation: it was June 4. That day happened to be Friday, the Feast of the Sacred Heart, and I rejoiced at this coincidence. It seemed to me that the Heart of Jesus himself had come to take the place of my heart by conferring on me his own Spirit. I was deeply moved by the thought that this sacrament is received only once in a lifetime and that it was going to make me a perfect Christian.

After this, the little girl lived in what seemed to her interminable anticipation of the liturgical feasts, when she was permitted once again to receive Holy Communion.

In October 1881, when it was Thérèse's turn to attend the Abbey, Céline showed more enthusiasm for her studies. She made the trip with her cousin Jeanne Guérin, leaving her younger sister to accompany Marie, up to the point when

[2] In her old age, Sister Geneviève was delighted to rediscover and meditate on this text that had once made such an impression on her.

Céline at the age of two, 1871

discussions between the older ones became sharp at times and the companions changed places. This was because Céline had become quarrelsome. She herself acknowledged having been "well able to defend myself", in the figurative sense, of course. It was not by physical force but "by the sword of the word" that she defended her point of view when she thought she was right—and "one is always right about some particular", she shrewdly observed.

She protected her little sister, who preferred to chatter ("*discourir*") rather than to run about ("*courir*") and who loathed rough games. She herself tried to overcome her own natural timidity since she was told it was a fruit of self-love. She retained enough of it, however, not to have the courage to present herself for her diploma.

At recess, when the class was divided into two sides for a little "war", Céline always had to be on the side of the French; otherwise, she intentionally let herself be beaten. When an assistant teacher of English origin spoke of Joan of Arc as an "adventuress", a hand was raised in protest—that of our Céline again, who, in addition, went in search of the headmistress of the boarding school and demanded that the teacher in question be reprimanded or else she would have her father intervene. M. Martin was not mistaken when he nicknamed her "the brave one", and "the intrepid".

Nevertheless, the child had a tender heart, thirsting for consolation. To be deprived of it because everyone thought she was strong was always a severe trial for her. She experienced this with a lady to whom she was deeply attached. Not seeing this attachment reciprocated, she wept bitterly. She later recognized this as a visible protection of her by God, who wanted to keep her for himself alone.

Céline and Thérèse blossomed fully only at Les Buissonnets. The manuscript of *The Story of a Soul* obligingly tells about their play, the care lavished on their large birdcage, the family outings, the walks on Sundays and feast days. We see them dressed up as pilgrims, armed with a stick to ward off the pecking of a chattering magpie and walking around the garden forty times. On their respective feast days, they would spend ten sous on surprise gifts, which they offered to each other. One particular day Céline took it into her head to bestow upon her sister a toy gun, which frightened her and which M. Martin then presented to a neighborhood boy, not without reimbursing his "little Queen".

"I had been given the title of 'Céline's little girl'," recounted Thérèse in her autobiography, "so when she was annoyed with me, the greatest sign of her displeasure was to say to me: 'You are no longer my little girl; that's over, and I'll always remember it! . . .' Then all I had to do was cry like a Magdalen, begging her to look on me as her little girl again; soon she was kissing me and promising that she would remember nothing! . . . In order to console me, she took one of her dolls and said to it: 'My dear, give your aunt a kiss.' "

At times, with the children of the Guérin and Maudelonde families, they put on short plays in which poor Céline unfailingly had the wicked role. This never failed to humiliate her, for her friends took a malignant pleasure in calling her the names of the wretched characters she portrayed on stage. She consequently did not like these parlor games and preferred the processions where, dressed in white, she appeared next to Thérèse with a basket of flowers in her hands.

J'amais aussi, petite fille,
Devant l'ostensoir qui scintille,
Jeter bien haut roses, lys et jonquilles,
Mêlant à celles de ma sœur
Mes fleurs.

Little girl, 'tis my delight
Before the monstrance shining bright
To toss roses, lilies, jonquils high,
Letting my flowers
Mingle with those of my sister.

The departure of Pauline for the cloister in October 1882 threw a veil of sadness over the calm life of Les Buissonnets. For Céline, this separation was even more painful since it was followed so soon by Thérèse's illness. She shared in her anguish; she prayed by her side and was able to gaze upon her ecstatic face when the smile of the Virgin Mary cured her. She also witnessed her fervent preparation for her first Holy Communion. It was she who, during Thérèse's retreat at the Abbey, brought the picture to her that so enchanted her: the Flower of the Divine Prisoner.

At the end of the school year of 1885, Céline completed her course of studies. She left the boarding school with honors, carrying off the prize in religious instruction, the only one for the whole institution and certainly the most coveted. She was received as a Child of Mary on December 8, 1882, and became in due time president of the association.

Freed from her studies, she nevertheless led a very active life. Jeanne Guérin, who was amazed at seeing how well she drew without having had any special training in it, obtained M. Martin's consent for her to take lessons. For two years, Céline made rapid progress. Eventually the time came to perfect her talent, and she was entrusted to Mlle. Godard, pupil of the artist Léon Cogniet. With much persistence, she worked methodically, alone in her studio, executing numerous copies, some seascapes, and a few portraits, which would fill her "museum of badly painted pictures", as she called it, but which taught her how to handle her tools.

Céline and Thérèse at the ages of twelve and eight, 1881

In addition, Marie, who was preparing for her entrance into the convent, initiated her into the running of the household. Céline took over with ease in October 1886, when Marie joined Pauline in the cloister while Léonie made her first attempt with the Poor Clares at Alençon.

III. The Sister of Thérèse's Soul

The family circle was becoming smaller. Henceforth, Céline and Thérèse were the only ones left to keep M. Martin company. More than ever they became spiritual sisters. Their life was very much regulated: "Nothing is left to one's whim." In the morning, there was Mass at 7:00 no matter what the weather. If ice turned the road from Les Buissonnets into a skating rink, they wrapped their shoes with cloth, but the weather did not make them miss their eucharistic celebration. Study and work around the house kept them busy during the day. On feast days, they organized some treat for the poor children in the neighborhood. If a beggar showed up, he was introduced and given something to eat, and the young girls knelt down to receive his blessing.

The "conversion" of Thérèse on December 25, 1886, giving her complete mastery over her sensitivity and drying the tears that flowed too easily, opened a new period in the relationship between the two sisters. The Saint noted with an acuity not devoid of humor:

> Céline had become the intimate confidante of my thoughts; since Christmas we could understand each other; the distance of age no longer existed since I had grown in height and above all in grace. . . . Before this period, I had often complained about not knowing Céline's secrets, and she told me I was too little, that I would have to grow "as high as a stool" so that she could put her

trust in me. . . . I loved to climb up on that precious stool when I was beside her and tell her to talk intimately to me, but my effort was useless; a distance still separated us! . . . Jesus, who wanted us to advance together, formed bonds in our hearts that were stronger than blood. We became spiritual sisters.

Such is the origin of those conversations in the belvedere that are mentioned in Thérèse's autobiography and that Céline, in turn, attempted to analyze:

The union of our souls became so intimate that I will not even try to describe it in earthly language: it would spoil the charm of it. . . . Each evening, "our hands linked together", our gaze immersed in the immensity of the heavens, we talked about that Life that was never to end. . . . Where were we when, losing, so to speak, consciousness of ourselves, our voices faded into silence? . . . Where were we then? I wonder.

Alas! Suddenly we would find ourselves again on earth, but we were no longer the same; and, as if coming out of a bath of fire, our breathless souls no longer aspired to anything but to spread their flames. . . . Oh, what intoxication! Oh, what martyrdom!

As Thérèse says, these graces cannot remain without fruit, and Jesus was pleased to show her that her apostolic desires were acceptable to him through the very miraculous conversion of the unfortunate Pranzini. It was this same grace that was the starting point of a more intimate union between us, for it was on this occasion that she discovered in the heart of her Céline the beginning of the aspirations that were consuming her own.

Even allowing for youthful sensitivity, the fact remains that Céline underwent a profound change. She pondered her future. She already knew about the life of the Benedictines. Carmel did not yet attract her, although it crossed her mind. The intervention of Father Pichon would be a determining factor in her life. This Jesuit, born in 1843 in Carrouges, near Alençon, had become acquainted with the Martin family in

1882, after a retreat that Marie attended. Two years later, he was sent to Canada, and he returned in September 1886. It was then, in the visits he made to Les Buissonnets, that Céline had the opportunity to appreciate his qualities. On October 12, 1887, he became her spiritual director. Very exuberant and feeling the need to confide in someone, she regularly sent him her spiritual diary, to which he responded once or twice a year. He obviously appreciated her energetic personality, her straightforwardness, and even her "theology", as he called it. He declared one day laughingly that "she had life enough for all." Very austere with himself, to the point of always wearing a hair shirt, he preached above all confident devotion to the Sacred Heart and love of the Mass. He seems to have had a charism for directing people to the religious life, which at times alienated him from the sympathy of mothers of families.

Under his influence, Céline felt her inclinations strengthened. She had a true, deep, interior piety, quite capable, if necessary, of using trickery to "steal her God", to use her expression. Having, in fact, permission to receive communion several days a week in addition to feast days, she developed a very extensive exegesis of this permission, which her confessor, at the time the Abbé Baillon, obligingly overlooked. Whenever some trip prevented her from receiving communion as often as prescribed, she made up for it later and, if she lost count along the way, always concluded in her own favor in order to extend the permissions.

We can see, in this behavior, that there was nothing at all in her of what the world assesses as narrow and morose pietism. Nor anything conformist. Doing what everyone else did was never a valid argument for her. Before receiving communion, she removed her bracelet, because she considered it a "sign of servitude", while Christ wants free souls. She gladly hummed the ancient canticle: "Take my heart; there it is, O Virgin, my sweet Mother", but toned down the passage: "It is for its rest that it has recourse to thee." "What does this sentence mean?" she exclaimed. "As for me, it's because I love her."

It soon became apparent that she was made for religious life. Nevertheless, she stepped aside in view of Thérèse. In May 1887, M. Martin suffered a slight stroke. He recovered from it but could not be left alone. Céline would take care of the house and, if needed, act as his nurse. So with all her affection she supported the efforts of her young sister, who aspired to leave home forever at the age of fifteen.

"The love of God was so intense in my poor heart", she wrote, "that finding nothing that could bring even the least relief to this need I had of giving, I was happy to sacrifice all that I held most dear in the world. . . . Like Abraham, I busied myself with the preparation of the holocaust, and I helped my dear sister in all the steps she took to obtain her entrance into Carmel despite her great youth. I took her disappointments more to heart than if they had been my own."

The Saint underlined the merit of such abnegations:

It was, so to speak, the same soul that gave us life; for a few months, we'd enjoyed together the sweetest life that young girls could dream of; everything around us corresponded to our tastes; the greatest liberty was given us; I would say our life on earth was the ideal of happiness. . . . We scarcely had time to taste this ideal of happiness when it was necessary to turn away from it freely, and my dear Céline did not rebel even for an instant. Still, she was not the one whom Jesus was calling first, so she could have complained . . . , having the same vocation as I, it was her right to leave! . . . But as in the time of the martyrs, those who remained in prison would joyfully give the kiss of peace to their brothers leaving first to fight in the arena and were consoled with the thought that perhaps they had been saved for still greater combats; so Céline let her Thérèse go away, and she remained alone for the glorious and bloody combat to which Jesus destined her as the privileged one of his love!

Céline accompanied Thérèse to Rome, and it was she—thanks to the documents she so carefully gathered—who would permit the path for that journey to be established with certainty. Her artistic temperament was moved by the natural wonders amassed in the landscapes of Switzerland and Italy, the masterpieces of art, beyond the mountains, that filled the churches and the museums. She observed closely the Holy House of Loreto; she descended with her younger sister into the ruins of the Coliseum; with her she slipped into the depths of the ancient tomb of Saint Cecilia. And it was she above all who, during the papal audience when the pilgrims had just been reminded that they were to file by in silence before Leo XIII, encouraged her Thérèse by this one vigorous word: "Speak!" She herself confides to us the secret of this apparently insubordinate attitude: "I have one principle for such occasions, and that is always to follow in all points a resolution made in advance." Under the circumstances, who would dream of reproaching her for it?

She gave evidence of the same decisive spirit during the Lyons stage of their return trip, when an impressive-looking individual, aglitter with medals, started a discussion with the two sisters about their journey to the Eternal City, congratulating them on such a privilege, but slipping into the praise a bit of irony regarding the Pope, calling him a "powerless old man". Céline sprang forward in response: "One might wish, sir, that you were his age; perhaps then you might also have his experience, which would keep you from speaking thoughtlessly of things you know nothing about."

During the course of this excursion through the mountains, the intimacy between Thérèse and Céline was such that their traveling companions said of them: "Those young girls are never separated from each other." Separation came about, however, when on Monday, April 9, 1888, the little Queen, after attending Mass together at the Carmel with her family, left them to rejoin her older sisters in the cloister. "While kissing her goodbye at the monastery door," wrote Céline, "I had to support myself unsteadily against the wall . . . and yet, I did not cry; I wanted to give her to Jesus with all my heart; and he, in return, clothed me with his strength! Ah! How I needed that divine strength! At the moment when Thérèse stepped into that Holy Ark, the door of the cloister that closed between us was the faithful image of what really happened, for a wall was raised between our two lives."

The wall did not exist for Thérèse, who, on the following May 8, wrote to her sister:

> Tomorrow it will be a month that I am far from you, but it seems to me that we are not separated; what does the place matter where we are! . . . Even if the ocean separated us, we would remain united, for our desires are the same, and our hearts beat together. . . . I am sure you understand me. After all, what does it matter whether life is pleasant or sad; we would come nonetheless to the end of our journey here below. A day of a Carmelite spent without suffering is a day lost; it is the same for you, because you are a Carmelite at heart.

2

The Filial Mission of Céline

I. The Great Trial

Céline had scarcely completed the heartrending act that separated her from Thérèse when she found herself confronted with a totally different kind of trial: a request for marriage, in due and proper form, the logical outcome of maneuvers that the young girl thought she had cleverly thwarted. Without being actually pretty, she was charming, which is even better. Of average height, lively like her mother, with a vivacious spirit and ready rejoinders, she created around her a bright and joyful atmosphere. Her eyes were of surprising depth, searching and probing, and at the same time attracted others with a flash of mischievous good humor. She had many talents. A notary public once said to M. Martin about her: "You needn't provide a dowry for that one; she carries her fortune at her fingertips." Obviously, she did not pass by unnoticed.

The crisis was painful. She wrote in her autobiography:

This piece of news distressed me, not that I was undecided as to what I had to do, but the divine light, in hiding itself from me, delivered me up to my own fickleness; I kept telling myself: "Isn't this offer, which is made to me the instant Thérèse leaves me, an indication of God's will for me, which I hadn't foreseen?" The Lord may have permitted me this desire for religious life up until now so that, in the world, I might be a strong woman. So many people tell me I do not have the makings of a religious! Perhaps, indeed, I haven't been called to that life by divine Providence. My sisters never had to choose formally between the two lives; doubtless, God wanted them for himself, and he does not want me! In short, although my resolution had never changed, my anguish kept mounting and mounting. . . . I could no longer see clearly. Yet, just in case, I responded that I was not willing, that I wanted to be left in peace for the time being, and that no one should wait for me.

Céline's confessor, Canon Delatroëtte, pastor of Saint-Jacques and ecclesiastical superior of the Carmel, did not intervene in this matter. Father Pichon, whom she saw again on the occasion of Marie's profession on May 22, approved and strengthened her resolution.

Other concerns were not long in absorbing the young girl's attention. Her father showed alarming signs of cerebral arteriosclerosis: forgetfulness, anxiety, and hallucinations that, even though short-lived, made her fear more serious difficulties nonetheless. In the course of one of his trips to Paris to take care of some business matters, he rented a villa in Auteuil. His intention was to give Céline the opportunity to perfect her artistic talent by frequenting the Academies and profiting by the lessons of some master. This is what he proposed to her on Saturday, June 16, 1888, when she showed him, in the belvedere, one of her paintings depicting the Virgin and the Magdalen. Her answer was not long in coming. "Without taking time to think about it," confided Céline, "I set down the picture I was holding in my hand and, drawing near to Father, I confided to him that since I wanted to be a religious I did not seek the glory of the world, that if God needed my works later on, he could very well make up for my ignorance. I added that I preferred my innocence to all other advantages and that I did not want to risk it in artists' studios."

M. Martin had sensed the vocation of his daughter. Never before, however, had she spoken to him openly. Very much moved, he pressed her to his heart and said: "Come, let us go together close to the Blessed Sacrament to thank God for the honor that he has given me by asking for all of my children." He said he was prepared for an immediate separation. "You can all leave. I will be happy to give you to God before I die. In my old age, a bare cell will be enough for me."

God was demanding more. His health continued to deteriorate; the old gentleman found himself caught once again by his dreams of the eremitical life: to flee far from his family, in solitude, so that his daughters could realize their destiny. Possessed by these thoughts, he left Lisieux without warning on June 23, 1888. After she had spent three days looking anxiously for him, a telegram sent from Le Havre and asking for a reply to be sent "general delivery" enabled Céline and M. Guérin to catch up with him and bring him home.

In the meantime, to the great terror of Léonie,[1] a fire had destroyed the house next door, threatening for a time their own dear home. All was restored to order. M. Martin bought the disaster-stricken building for the purpose of enlarging Les Buissonnets, which he planned to purchase.

From the first to the fifteenth of July, they stayed at Auteuil. It was not a happy diversion for them because their hearts felt uprooted so far from Carmel; and the lease was canceled. Through all these events and emotions, the sick man became more and more appreciative of Céline's devotion. He readily made her a gift of a beautiful copper crucifix that Marie had given him for a keepsake before she left for the cloister and that was particularly dear to his heart.

[1] Léonie had returned home on January 6, 1888, from her second unsuccessful attempt at religious life.—Ed.

On August 12, he suffered another relapse, followed by several weeks of calm. Before Father Pichon sailed to Canada, which had once again been assigned as the field for his missionary work, M. Martin, with his two daughters, wanted to greet him at Le Havre on October 31. Passing through Honfleur, he experienced one of his darkest days. Céline sought refuge in the church of Notre-Dame de Grâce. The same day, she wrote to her Carmelites: "No words, no expression could ever tell our anguish, our heartbreak. I feel so powerless. Dear little sisters, my suffering was so acute that, while walking along the edge of the wharf, I looked with envy into the depths of the water. Ah! if I did not have faith, I would be capable of anything." She became calm at last in the love of Christ crucified. "It is not a little cross that he lays on our shoulders but his own. . . . We are not working for ourselves but for him. I find great consolation in this thought. For him! Oh! that we might give to him, give to him without ceasing, until the last breath of our life!"

On November 3, since M. Martin had recovered sufficiently and Father Pichon had never arrived, the three travelers returned to the capital. Life began anew, mixed with hopes and anxieties, until January 10, 1889, the day when Thérèse received the habit, which was for her and for all her family an unclouded feast, like a "Palm Sunday" before the great Passion.

The month had not passed when alarming news came again. Céline sent to Carmel this note in which supernatural optimism tries at all costs to keep the upper hand:

> Beloved little sisters, I am calling to mind these words of the *Imitation*: "I will give infinite glory for a single short-lived humiliation. . . ." Oh! humiliations! They are our daily bread, but if only you knew what I see hidden in them! . . . To me, it is a mystery of love.

O my little sisters, do not be grieved, I pray you; has Thérèse prayed in vain? Is it in vain that I have placed some of the oil from the lamp of the Holy Face on the forehead of papa with so much confidence? No, a thousand times no! There is, I am sure, some wonderful purpose in all this that we cannot understand. I feel that our Lord is so very pleased when we have unlimited confidence in him, finding all that he does good. . . .

No, I am not going to ask God to relieve me of the humiliations, misunderstandings, heartaches, anxieties, bitterness. . . . But I do beg God to take all that away from our dear little father. He can grant us this grace, and I am sure that he will.

It became increasingly apparent that the state of health of him whom they liked to call "the Patriarch" required special care. Susceptible to congestive attacks, which were doubtlessly complicated by the onset of uremia, he was subject to mental lapses, during which he was in danger of running away or making irresponsible business decisions. M. Guérin insisted he be placed in Bon Sauveur in Caen. The young girls had to face the facts of the reasons cited. Nevertheless, the blow was cruel. The date of February 12, 1889[2]—"Our great treasure", as Thérèse called it in a spirit of faith—was written on Céline's calendar as a day of tears. At that time, when cures in a psychiatric institution were most infrequent, any transfer of this kind was interpreted in a derogatory way. The remarks that followed added to the humiliation. Certain people never missed an opportunity to speak of "mystical ravings" and attributed the source of this illness to that series of vocations inflicted on the powerless father.

In order to be near their father, Céline and Léonie returned the very next day to Caen and stayed with the Sisters

[2] In a touching coincidence, it was on this very date of February 12, and without anyone having thought of it beforehand, that the completion of the Diocesan Process in view of the Cause of M. Martin was pronounced in 1960.

of Saint Vincent de Paul. They could see their father only once a week, but every day they inquired about him from Sister Costard, who was in charge of the department where he was located.

> The first time [wrote Céline] we saw our dear little father again, his reaction was such that he had several rather good days. He was then able to understand the whole situation and generously made his sacrifice. God is permitting this in order to give him the entire merit of his trial. The doctors of the establishment told him one day while lavishing their care on him that they were going to cure him, but he answered: "Oh! I don't want that; I even ask God not to hear the prayers of those who make that intention, because this trial is a mercy. I am here to atone for my pride. I deserve the illness that has struck me down!" The doctors could not believe their ears, and the sister who related this conversation to me was so moved that she still had tears in her eyes. "We have never seen the like", she said to us; "we're caring for a saint."

Even in the most difficult moments, M. Martin was entirely resigned; he showed gentleness and an unfailing charity to those around him. He even wanted to continue his mortifications; he shared with others the little treats heaped upon him and received communion as often as possible. Those around him were moved at seeing the mark of so much suffering on his venerable face.

The cruelest blow for the sick man was the blundering intervention of certain lawyers who, overstepping orders they had received, had him sign a waiver relinquishing the management of his own affairs. They protected themselves by saying it was the wish of the entire family: "Ah! it is my children who are abandoning me!" the old man sobbed. And he yielded immediately. Sister Geneviève, who relates this, adds: "I cannot begin to tell you what this new wound did to my heart . . . it was the worst yet. This time, the point of the

Louis Martin, the father of Thérèse and Céline, in a wheelchair after his paralytic stroke, surrounded by (l. to r.) Marie Guérin, Léonie Martin, a servant, Céline, a servant, M. Isidore Guérin, and, in the foreground, the family dog, "Tom"

sword had reached the last fibers; our souls were pierced through and through."

In response to the letters from Carmel, which were full of encouragement, the young girl kept Lisieux informed about the state of his health and confessed alternately to dejection and to hope. "At that moment, bitterness invaded my heart; I placed everything in the hands of Jesus, and he is taking care of it. How was that done? I know nothing about it; Jesus came to our aid."

Thoughts of eternity, so familiar to her parents, haunted her more than ever. In the musical rhythm of Lamennais' prose, she could see her mother calling for "the Homeland". She recalled the chapters of the Abbé Arminjon on "The Mysteries of the Life Beyond" and the glorious return of Christ saying to his friends, at last delivered from their distress: "Now, it's my turn!"

"The longer I live," she wrote on February 27, "the more I see exile on all sides. The world seems like a dream to me, immense confusion. . . . The more I travel, and the more I see of things, the more detached I am from this earth, because, at each instant, the more I observe the nothingness of what passes away. I am in a real cell; nothing pleases me more than this poverty. I would not exchange it for the most brilliant drawing room in the world." She confided to Mother Marie de Gonzague that her only happiness was the chapel, where she spent all her time outside of work; yet, she prayed without relish and at times fell asleep at the feet of Jesus.

Suffering accepted in this manner is an uphill climb. In this rough apprenticeship, the soul is refined and purified. We can sense this in the letter of March 1, 1889:

> Little sisters, I want to be happy about our tribulations and to do even more: to thank God for the bitterness of our humiliations. I do not know why, but instead of receiving these trials with bitter-

ness and complaint, I see something mysterious and divine in the conduct of our Lord toward us! Besides, did he himself not pass through all humiliations? . . . I admit that the opinion of others means nothing to me.

Ah! if you knew how I see God in all our trials! Yes, everything in them bears the visible imprint of his divine finger.

It was in this spirit that the daughters of M. Martin had a marble plaque bearing this inscription installed in the chapel of the Carmel under the image of the Holy Face:[3]

Sit Nomen Domini Benedictum
F. M.
1888

As early as March 3, M. Guérin insisted that his nieces return to Lisieux. Céline resisted. "I feel more and more that my duty is to remain here; yes, it is better to suffer and not abandon our dear little father; at least, here, if we can do nothing for him, we feel quite close to him and can rush to him at a moment's notice." It had to be recognized, however, that this exodus could not be prolonged indefinitely. The health of the two young girls was in danger of being jeopardized. Upon the further insistence of their uncle, they went back to Les Buissonnets on May 14, 1889.

It was not for long. On June 7, they took board and lodging at the home of M. Guérin, who, after receiving a handsome legacy, had given up his pharmaceutical practice and

[3] The inscription means, "Blessed be the Name of the Lord." Later, Sr. Geneviève would return with emotion to this offering of a plaque commemorating their father's great trial. "To the voices that spoke to us then of a 'bleak future', the Church now responds that she is preparing to place one of us on her altars. We gave a marble offering to God, and now we do not have enough space to collect those addressed to his little servant, Thérèse of the Child Jesus."

from this time on lived in a huge mansion on the rue Paul-Banaston. On December 25, the lease on Les Buissonnets expired. Céline tells about the last visit she made to the old house, plucking, instead of flowers, "some ivy leaves . . . a souvenir of so many memories". She speaks with a melancholy air about the dispersal of the household, one part going to Carmel, with Tom, the faithful dog, following behind the carriage and slipping in through a half-open door to bombard a much-moved Thérèse with his endearments.

II. Confronting the Dangers of the World

They adapted to their new life. Mme. Guérin, who was kindness itself, had a rather admiring affection for Céline. With M. Guérin, good Christian that he was, of magnificent integrity but an unyielding and imperious character, there were sometimes clashes as Céline was the only one who could argue with him—undoubtedly because they were of the same stock. But they loved each other nonetheless. It was as a family that they worked, relaxed, visited the Exposition in Paris, and went to Lourdes and Spain.

In the morning, after daily Mass, where she always received communion—which never ceased to disturb her aunt's timid cautiousness—Céline devoted herself to her painting, executing, among other things, some pictures for Carmel: the Adoration of the Shepherds, Saint John of the Cross, and other subjects, as well as some small pieces of artistic work. She also used children and old men to pose as models for her; they were happy to be generously paid and treated with respect. In the afternoon she did needlework, making clothes for the poor, or sometimes taught catechism to slow learners or the retarded. The young girl's down-to-earth mind together with her lively imagination, which illustrated the most abstract lessons with anecdotes, worked wonders in her teaching. One of her protégés protested once when he was placed with another teacher. Ten years later, he returned to ask the "good lady" for the notebook she had fashioned for him in which to mark down his sacrifices in preparation for his First Communion and which, through childish carelessness, he had neglected to get back from her at the time.

Reading also took up a large share of Céline's day. She had a wide range of interests, from Plato to literary authors, all the way through works of chivalry, religious writings, and scientific journals. She had a thirst for learning that, on the advice of Father Pichon, she had to moderate somewhat. At times, her choice was photography and electroplating. Céline tried her hand at everything. She did not hesitate to take apart and put back together again, piece by piece, a sewing machine that needed adjusting. She also memorized a whole anthology of poetry and in the evening gladly listened to her uncle recite selected passages from the classics. It was self-taught education that would leave its mark on her forever.

She explored the Old Testament, especially the Wisdom books and the Prophets; she drew from them a whole series of excerpts, which, carefully copied, filled the fifty-six pages of a notebook she compiled. An anthology, along the same lines although more concise, was filled with verses from the Book of Revelation and other selected quotations from various spiritual writers.

God remained for her the "one thing necessary". Not satisfied with the delight of reading fine biographies that strengthened her in this conviction, she tackled heavy treatises that unveiled the secrets of asceticism and opened onto mystical heights. Father Surin, John of the Cross, Teresa of Avila,

Henry Suso, Father d'Argentan each in turn served as masters for consideration.

In order to remain faithful to the Lord, she had to struggle. Witness this retrospective admission that opens the notebook of her eightieth year: "I look upon my soul as a fortified castle that was extraordinarily coveted by the enemy. The object of endless dangerous attacks, perilous assaults, and extreme wars. Certainly, I have suffered much, but my Jesus, my Divine Cavalier, faithful to his Lady, has fought for me, and he has won."

The recently ousted suitor had not given up the fight. Others appeared on the horizon. Céline could not cut herself off totally from social functions, which were frequent at the home of the Guérins. The devil had a hand in it; for more than two years she underwent violent temptations that tormented her mind and imagination in particular and left her no respite. She would sit on the chest of drawers in her room and grasp the body of the statue of the Virgin that had smiled on Thérèse. She meditated, verse by verse, on the beautiful Psalm 90(91) of Sunday's Compline, which sings of the invincible aid of the Most High: "*Qui habitat in adjutorio altissimi*". At certain times, weary and as if tired of herself, she thought she was damned. Her health was shaken by it. Suffering from stomach and heart trouble, she consulted Doctor Notta. Letters from Father Pichon, although rare, brought her some relief. In general, he confined himself to confirming the points of view that she set forth in all candor and that revealed a very sound judgment. On December 8, 1889, the young girl made a vow of chastity, which she renewed annually. "It is Jesus who has gained the victory", she concluded each time calm was restored within her.

The long interior drama, which contributed to her detachment, did not prevent her from being the surest of counselors herself for her young cousin Marie, who was being assailed by scruples. She encouraged her to receive communion. She helped her in her search for perfection, which did not please her parents greatly, little inclined as they were to favor the awakening of a religious vocation, which they nevertheless would approve in due time.

Céline's focus of attention was the monastery on the rue de Livarot, where she hoped to join her sisters. On this subject, she was inexhaustible.

Carmel was everything for me. Each week, I went there to reimmerse myself in it near to my Thérèse. Léonie took her place to the right side of the grille with Pauline and Marie, and I sat at the left with my little sister. It was only at the end of the visit that the conversation became general.

I could never receive enough advice from my dear Thérèse. I consulted her in everything. . . . How our souls were united! I found my family again there, and my heart was warmed by this contact. We were birds of a feather. We talked about our dear father. The same things interested us, the same joys and the same sorrows made our hearts beat.

Thérèse's manuscript conveys the same idea: "Ah! far from separating us, the grilles of Carmel united our souls more closely; we had the same thoughts, the same desires, the same love of Jesus and souls. . . . When Céline and Thérèse spoke to each other, never did a word about the things of the earth mingle in their conversations, which were already in heaven. Like before in the belvedere, they dreamed about the things of eternity, and, in order to enjoy this endless happiness soon, they chose 'suffering and contempt' as their portion here below."

The exchange of letters reiterated these conversations. The only regular occasions for this correspondence were Céline's birthday, on April 28, and the feast day of her patroness, virginal companion of St. Geneviève and protectress of the village of Meaux, on October 21. Always the cunning one, the young girl was very careful to give up a visit to her sisters as these fateful days approached. She wanted "her letter". Only afterward did she go to say thank you, which was always one more joy and blessing.

Her cleverness in this matter earned us a packet of forty-five letters that constitute human documents of prime importance. In them, the Saint slips imperceptibly from the role of friend and sister to that of mother. Little by little the confidante establishes herself as authentic spiritual guide. Before their father was institutionalized, Thérèse consoled Céline, who dreaded the fatal outcome. In opening her own heart, Thérèse directed her to accept it in pure faith.

> Life is often burdensome. What bitterness, but what sweetness! . . . If we feel Jesus present! oh! we would really do everything for him . . . but no, he seems a thousand leagues away, we are all alone with ourselves; oh! what annoying company when Jesus is not there! But what is this gentle Friend doing then? Does he not see our anguish? . . . He is not far; he is there, very close, looking at us, begging us for this sadness, this agony. . . . He needs it for souls, for our soul (July 23, 1888).

When the cross became heavier, her exhortation was more urgent: "Why be afraid you cannot carry this cross without weakening?" Thérèse wrote in January 1889. "Jesus, on the road to Calvary, fell three times, and you, poor little child, would you not be like your Spouse, would you not be willing to fall a hundred times, if necessary, in order to prove your love for him, rising with greater strength than before your fall? . . ."

The trial was prolonged; temptations to discouragement threatened to overwhelm her. On her return from a visit at Bon Sauveur, Céline let a moan escape. This was in April 1889.

How my poor heart is broken! I cannot get used to seeing our dear little father so ill. I always remember how it was at home, when he spoke to us like a true patriarch. He is so good!

Oh! how God must love us in seeing us so afflicted! I ask myself why he is not impatient to call our beloved father to himself; it seems to me that he is making a great effort to leave him here on earth; some great good will have to come of it, both for his own glory as well as for papa and for us; without that, he could not wait so long. . . . Dear little sisters, how happy we shall be when we are all reunited again on high! How these trials make us sigh for our heavenly home!

Thérèse answered on April 26, inviting her sister to carry her cross even if feebly. She paraphrased or quoted verbatim a few thoughts from Father Pichon: "Jesus suffered in sadness; without sadness, would the soul suffer?" "It is only when the saints were at our Lord's feet that they found their cross."

These excerpts gave Céline a taste for the teachings of the holy Jesuit, and she wanted to see the notebook in which Sister Marie of Saint Joseph had collected the essence of his instruction. It was less than a verbatim transcription but more than a summary. The teaching, accompanied by anecdotes and quotations from the best religious writers, was entirely oriented toward humility, confidence in the Sacred Heart, love of suffering, abandonment, and joy. Céline applied herself to recopying the whole text in her small, very distinctive handwriting. And so we have a notebook ruled with squares, 144 pages of thirty-two lines each, with extremely dense writing: a true little volume that bears witness to the supernatural eagerness and courageous tenacity of the one who imposed such an effort on herself.

She had great need of this nourishment to preserve her peace. Once a week, she went to Caen with Léonie to visit her father. In October 1890, when Jeanne Guérin would marry Francis La Néele, who would open his medical practice in that city, the two of them would be able to stay for longer periods of time. The state of the old gentleman remained unchanged, with occasional clear intervals that rekindled their hopes. They had expected his presence at Thérèse's clothing on September 24, but M. Guérin opposed it at the last moment, fearing that the emotion could be fatal. This cast a gloom over the whole ceremony.

When his legs became paralyzed, the "Patriarch", who no longer required special surveillance and who proved, moreover, to be of unfailing gentleness, was able to be brought back to Lisieux. On May 10, 1892, he was transferred to the rue Labbey, near the home of his brother-in-law. Céline lovingly reassumed her duties as his nurse along with the responsibilities of managing the house. Léonie's presence at their side would be only intermittent, for the young girl, who had accompanied Céline on a pilgrimage to Paray-le-Monial, had felt the call to religious life awaken within her once again. On June 23, 1893, she made a second try at the Visitation convent in Caen.

How did Céline understand her task? A passage from her spiritual notebook tells us:

> My joy was great at being able to care for my beloved father myself. . . . I never grew tired of embracing him; I showed him my affection in a thousand different ways and did everything I could to please him. He was interested in everything going on around him. And above all, he loved to hear my cousin Marie play the piano and stayed to listen to her.

Yet, it became necessary to set up their own household.

> My uncle spoke highly of a residence near his own. Ah! It was not Les Buissonnets! But the box did not matter; we possessed the "fine pearl"! And I was so happy that even to stay in a dungeon with him

would have seemed sheer delight to me. Nothing, nothing would have made any difference to me in his company. . . . No, it was not ordinary filial love that I had for my father; I repeat, it was a kind of worship.

The staff working there caused some concern. Later, Sister Geneviève of the Holy Face spoke about it good-humoredly. She told also of the emotion she felt at the end of a novena to Saint Joseph for the conversion of one of the servants when she saw this person fall at her feet and humbly confide: "I am a miserable wretch; for many years I have been separated from God, I have committed sacrileges, but I want to change. It is just now, while looking at the picture of the Blessed Virgin, that my heart melted like wax." The young girl referred him to Canon Rohée, archpriest of Saint-Pierre, who did not hide his edification at such a conversion. The picture in question (and the coincidence made an impression on Céline) was the same canvas she had presented to her father on June 16, 1888, and that had given her the opportunity to confide her vocation to him.

A few months earlier, in 1891, Céline intervened to persuade her uncle to set the journal *Le Normand* on its feet again and to assume its direction. He was hesitating, and his wife even more so, sensing strongly that this would threaten their peace. In a curious detail that reveals something about the period, he particularly dreaded, in his honor as a man as well as in his Christian conscience, possible challenges to a duel. His niece, with her usual spirit, swept away the objection. There were the interests of God and the Church, which *Le Progrès Lexovien* was holding up to ridicule throughout its columns. "Well! You have won, my big-hearted girl", concluded the former pharmacist who was becoming an impromptu journalist. Céline was also the first to congratulate him on an admirable article in which

La Musse, the summer home of the Guérin family

he avenged Leo XIII for the base attacks of a young politician.

M. Guérin had become a prominent figure in Lisieux. Thus it was that he became acquainted with M. Krug, a well-known artist, originally from Normandy and a student of Flandrin. He invited him to give lessons to Céline, who derived a great deal of profit from such training. Under the supervision of this master, she tackled some subjects that were difficult to execute. He praised her highly for her skill at composition and was committed to introducing her to the Salon [an annual art exhibition in Paris] if she would consent to take some courses of study in the capital. (The young girl did not hesitate to climb up the scaffolding in order to admire, at close range, the frescoes with which her patron was adorning the choir of the Abbey.) On several occasions, M. Krug went to see her at Carmel to inspect her progress, which gave her more confidence. He even offered her his large palette.

Céline did not allow herself to become dazzled by success of this kind. Thérèse had introduced her to the devotion to the Holy Face. She had her meditate on the humiliation of the suffering Messiah as found in the prophet Isaiah. After such reflections, how could the world not be a burden? She shared the thirst for souls that devoured her young sister. With her she prayed and sacrificed herself for the once-brilliant preacher at Notre Dame, Father Hyacinthe Loyson, who gave up his religious vows and left the priesthood.

Each summer, the young girl accompanied the Guérin family to the summer home, La Musse, near Evreux. It was a huge house in an imposing location, surrounded by almost one hundred acres of entirely enclosed parks and woods. Life there was joyous and varied: games, parties, excursions, with all the delights of comfort and the pleasures of friendship.

Céline did not let this turn her head. Rather, she experienced the boredom of such luxury. She could barely tolerate being waited on. Like her mother before her, she aspired to the great restoration that would be accomplished in heaven, where artificial inequities would cease and where each one would be treated according to his true worth. Surprised at herself for leaning back so indolently on the cushions in the carriage that took her visiting, she felt overcome with great contempt for herself. "Is it really I, the proud and independent one, who plays a part in this comedy! My Jesus himself glories in hiding himself after having surrounded all his works with mystery!" She immediately lost her fondness for a bracelet she had just purchased: "What! I would have a chain fastened to my wrist! Am I then a slave?"

The occasions for *divertissement* (entertainment), in the Pascalian sense of the term, were many. In the evenings Céline, by her spirited conversation, was the main attraction. She could not undo her naturally pleasing personality, much less disguise it, so she was the most sought after. The attentions lavished on her increased to the point that M. Guérin, totally unaware of her future plans, thought it his duty to put her on her guard. In fact, she had a horror of these marks of attention. She refused several marriage proposals. Since she was not able to avoid these social gatherings, she prepared for them by prayer and went to them equipped with a crucifix that she squeezed every now and then in her hand. She suggested the same tactic to a somewhat giddy friend, at the same time inviting her to dress more modestly. When people talked to her about worldly things, she would change the subject. When asked her opinion, she gave it honestly. We know, from Thérèse's manuscript, about the episode of the unsuccessful dance, when Céline and her partner felt powerless to waltz. He slipped away, completely downcast, while Céline was the first to laugh at the curious experience. This episode, which took place at the wedding of M. Henry Maudelonde, nephew of Mme. Guérin, shows us how Céline was visibly protected by the prayers of her sister, who felt she had been entrusted spiritually with a great mission in her regard.

If she put on a show of amiability to those around her, she nonetheless suffered from surroundings so ill matched to the ideal she was pursuing. Communion each morning as well as the daily hour of prayer sustained her. During the final period, she fixed up a very austere, bare room for herself, where she was able to forget the life of a lady of leisure. She also liked to escape with her cousin Marie to visit the poor or arrive at some neighboring church whose neglected state grieved her.

> I saw [she wrote] our wealthy and spacious home, adorned with gold paneling and silken tapestries; and looking out over the valley I noticed, in the distance, the dusty steeple denoting the earthly home of our God. Yes, he lived nearby, and I have seen him in his tabernacle, in a repulsive, dark, and dirty corner. . . . While my personal keys were gilt, his were all rusty and ground into a miserable lock supported by worm-eaten wood. What a shame to live in a sumptuous building when Jesus dwells in a hovel!

Céline suffered no less to see the contrast between this luxury and the indigence of the poor. "I thought back to my childhood, when I used to visit my little Thérèse at the home of her nurse, and we were ushered into the one and only room, which served as the kitchen, bedroom, and parlor all at the same time. The floor was hard-packed earth. . . . I reflected that truth and freedom, and therefore happiness, dwelled under the old dark beams rather than under artistic ceilings, and I looked forward to the happy moment when I would be transplanted to a poor cell."

Even though she preferred the thatched hut to the palace, the young girl did not have any less of an appreciation for the landscape of La Musse. Thérèse took advantage of this to make her climb still higher:

> The vast solitudes, the enchanting horizons that open out before you must be speaking at great length to your soul. I myself do not see all that, but I do say with Saint John of the Cross:
>
> I have in my Beloved the mountains,
> The lonely wooded valleys. . . .
> And this Beloved instructs my soul, he speaks to it in silence, in darkness.

The Saint felt responsible for the vocation of her sister:

> The most intimate of my desires, the greatest of them all, which I thought would never be realized, was the entrance of my dear Céline into the same Carmel as ours. . . . This dream seemed unlikely to me: to live under the same roof, to share the joys and sorrows of my childhood companion; and so I made my sacrifice complete. I had confided to Jesus the future of my dear sister, resolved to see her leave for the ends of the world if necessary. The only thing that I could not accept was her not being the spouse of Jesus, for since I loved her as much as I loved myself, it was impossible for me to see her give her heart to a mortal being.

III. Her Vocation

In Lisieux, it was easier to flee frivolous social engagements. Another difficulty beset Céline, however. As early as June 1891, Father Pichon had written from Canada: "I think I'm going to need you for a great work later on." He gradually revealed to her a plan for a kind of secular institute, in centers called Bethany, whose work was to prepare for their first

Holy Communion children who had been morally neglected and to propagate good reading material among the people. He set forth their initial achievements and frankly urged her to take charge of the new foundation as soon as she was free. He further asked her not to say anything to her sisters about it. This order of silence weighed heavily upon the young girl. Her "singing soul" was now "melancholy". "I am in darkness, reduced to the state of a log", she wrote to Thérèse on August 17, 1892; "I scarcely think of Jesus; but perhaps, without noticing it, the log is being consumed under the ashes."

Without betraying her secret, she loyally told her sister about the prospect of a possible separation. This note of July 17, 1894, reveals a painful predicament.

> It seemed to me, I would be unable to tell you this very well, it seemed to me that you were too much to me, that you were a support to me that allowed me to depend on you too much, that I was relying on you too much, that you were too indispensable to me; in short, it seemed to me that in order to belong totally to God, it would be necessary to leave you. . . . I foresaw the future, and I believed I had to be separated from you in order to see you again only in heaven. I have had something like a presentiment of a sacrifice surpassing all other sacrifices.

This period of uncertainty was particularly bitter. Céline turned to the statue of the Virgin who had cured the little Queen and whose marvelous smile she herself believed she saw through her tears on the evening of Friday, December 16, 1892. One of her poems would preserve the memory of that inexpressible grace.

At Carmel, they were disturbed by the anxiety tormenting the young girl, an anxiety she could not completely hide. That is doubtlessly why Father Pichon, in a letter sent from Canada to Thérèse on September 21, 1893, inserted this paragraph: "Cherish Céline; she deserves it. I know it better than you. Our Lord is leading her to the heights by a rugged and steep path."

This recommendation was altogether superfluous. Did not the Saint herself write to her sister: "I feel very united to my Céline; I do believe that God has not often made two souls who understand each other so well: never a discordant note. When the hand of Jesus touches one of the lyres, it makes the other vibrate at the same time."

The letters took on more and more the character of spiritual direction. Thérèse had Céline follow in her footsteps. She disclosed to her her "little way"; she called her "the little child of Jesus". With her skill at symbolizing everything, she sent to her, on April 28, 1894, an envelope containing a tiny keepsake. The envelope bore these words: "A little picture painted by little Thérèse for the twenty-fifth birthday of little Céline, with the permission of little Mother Prioress."

These consolations, which recalled the distant grace of Les Buissonnets, helped Céline accomplish her noble task up to the very end. An almost maternal sentiment was awakened in her soul for her humiliated father, who depended entirely on her care. Thérèse later translated these sentiments into the poem "The Canticle of Céline":

> I loved to overwhelm with affection
> My little Father in his old age.
> He was everything to me . . . happiness . . . child . . . wealth!
> Ah! I often kissed him
> Tenderly.

The end, however, was drawing near. In the beautiful summer of 1894, as in the preceding year, M. Guérin had wished to take his brother-in-law to La Musse. The invalid was given a room in a ground-floor wing, which gave him easy access to

"A large-hearted girl" — her uncle M. Guérin

the park in his little wheelchair. Amid the splendor of nature he seemed to gain new strength. He liked to linger in the shadow of the great trees. Céline gives a vivid description of one of these peaceful scenes:

> I will always remember his beautiful face when, in the evening, as night fell in the deep woods, we stopped to hear a nightingale: he listened . . . with what expression in his gaze! It was like an ecstasy, some inexpressible part of heaven was reflected in his features. Then after a good moment of silence, we were still listening, and I saw tears streaming down his dear cheeks. Oh! what a fine day!
>
> Since then, he's doing less well. This extraordinary consolation cannot last; and yet, in spite of it all, how sweet his last days are! Who would have thought it? The Lord is acting with ineffable goodness toward us!

Toward the end of July, the state of the invalid grew worse, and extreme unction was administered to him. On Sunday, July 29, a cardiac arrest carried him gently away. Céline, who never left his bedside, received the last breath of him whom she had cared for so devotedly. She shared these last moments with the Carmel: "In a voice filled with emotion, I recited the prayer: Jesus, Mary, Joseph. His glance was full of life, recognition, and tenderness; his mind was alert. In an instant, I again found my beloved father as he was five years ago, blessing me and thanking me."

At that time also, it was necessary to reveal Father Pichon's project to Thérèse. The Saint suffered from this disappointment, which made her shed more tears than she had ever shed before and caused her violent headaches. Yet, she was resigned in the face of the opposition raised here and there to the introduction of a fourth member of the same family to the narrow circle of Carmel.

Even if Mother Agnes of Jesus, elected prioress on February 20, 1893, wished to accept Céline, and if Mother Marie de Gonzague nobly acquiesced to it, they still ran up against the explicit veto from one of the chapter sisters, Sister Aimée of Jesus. Céline remained hesitant. Contemplative life attracted her. But was she not yielding in that way to natural family love? In this confusion, she prayed and asked others to pray. Soon light came. She consulted Father Pichon, who wrote to her on August 20: "Go then as quickly as you can to hide yourself in the desert, to take your place among the victims Jesus has chosen. I have no doubts. I no longer hesitate. God's will seems obvious to me. Let us make our sacrifice with a generous heart." Canon Delatroëtte, whom Céline visited, was also moved and gave his consent. Msgr. Hugonin[4] confirmed it without delay. As for Sister Aimée of Jesus, Thérèse asked God to incline her heart toward accepting Céline; she wanted it to be a sign that M. Martin had gone straight to heaven. Her prayer had hardly been formulated when the sister came "with tears in her eyes", offering her assent.

Things happened quickly then. Céline's entrance was set for September 14, 1894, Feast of the Exaltation of the Holy Cross. The devil attacked her from behind. He inspired her with sudden aversions: that habit from another age, that veil that enclosed your head, that stiff walk! . . . She, so in love with beauty, so jealous of her liberty! . . . But the postulant did not recoil from such trifles. As at the papal audience when she had said to her sister: "Speak", so now she said to herself: "March!" She refused to take into account any apprehensions or nightmares that disturbed her last nights in the world. The day before her entrance, she took to the monastery the statue of the Virgin of the Smile, which was placed in the room next to Thérèse's cell. Then, with her mind made up, she passed through the cloister door.

[4] Msgr. Flavien-Abel-Antoine Hugonin was the bishop of Bayeux.

The Nativity (detail) — painted by Céline, 1893

3

Céline in the Cloister at the School of Thérèse

I. Her Postulancy and Reception of the Habit

Hardly had the door closed behind her when she who would be called Marie of the Holy Face experienced an inexpressible peace. "All my temptations vanished", she writes; "the storm gave way to calm and the deepest serenity. I felt that at last I had found the place of my repose."

Mother Agnes of Jesus took her to the cell that she would occupy from then on. There, Thérèse took her hand to show her a piece of paper that had been placed on the pillow for her. It was a poem that ended with this verse:

> Come to us, little girl!
> My crown lacks one bright pearl.
> The Lord said to us, and we are all here
> To pluck you from the world on our wings of white
> Like birds on the branches pluck a flower bright.
> Oh, come to us! Come to us, dear!

I could not express my emotion [writes Céline] when, upon drawing near to read this poem, I recognized Papa's handwriting. . . . It was he who welcomed me to this dwelling where the love of Jesus had reserved a place for me. . . . At the sight of this, waves of gratitude pressed my heart, and the emotion made tears flow, something that grief and anguish had not been able to do.

I cannot say what took place in me at that first meeting with my dear sisters. We said hardly anything to each other. I sat down silently on the edge of my straw mattress, like a tired traveler who, after a long absence and having gone through innumerable perils, now stops to catch her breath upon arriving at her destination, not daring as yet to believe her good fortune.

The first days were much to her liking. The austere simplicity of the convent pleased the young girl. As an artist, she admired the spare lines of the Carmelite habit, the white mantle set off against the dark background of the habit. Yesterday's objections were quickly swept away. Thérèse introduced her to the horarium, the customs, the use of the breviary. Thérèse confided to Sister Marie of the Sacred Heart her pleasant surprise at finding in Céline all her former freshness without a trace of the complexities with which the world marks souls. The postulant entered fully and entirely into religious life, the beauty of which she would never cease to exalt. Would she not kiss the cloister door on each anniversary of her entrance into the monastery?

Inevitably, difficulties were not long in surfacing. The most unforeseen came first. It took Céline many weeks to get accustomed to her straw mattress. Since she did not get enough sleep at night, she dozed at times during Office, prayer, and adoration. These were occasions for painful and humiliating struggles. It took her more than a year to get used to the diet, particularly to the fish, milk, and starch, which constituted the basic staple of it and which she detested. Since the soles of her feet were sore, it was extremely tiring for her to stand at her place in choir. Her health was frail and remained so to the end of her life. She had stomach trouble and suffered frequently from toothaches. The postulancy, however, allowed for certain accommodations, and Céline came through victorious.

On February 5, 1895, she received the habit. Snow was falling, and a sheaf of lilies was sent to the heroine of the day by the most persistent of her previous suitors. The usual sermon was given by Canon Ducellier, former vicar of Saint Peter's and later Dean of Trévières. Its theme was this verse from the Song of Songs: "Winter is past, the rains have ceased, arise, my beloved, and come." The homilist included a magnificent eulogy of M. Martin, whose memory hovered over the festivities.

The new Carmelite recounted her impressions.

> During the ceremony, I received a particular grace of intimate union with my Beloved; I saw nothing of what was going on around me. The presence of the Bishop, the numerous clergy, the crowd of visitors, had all disappeared before my eyes; I was alone with Jesus . . . when suddenly, I was awakened from my interior silence by the singing of Compline, which was vibrant and full of spirit. The choir intoned the psalm: *Qui habitat in adjutorio Altissimi* [he who dwells in the shelter of the Most High], and I understood its meaning; each word fell on my soul like the pledge of a sacred promise made to me by the One to whom I had united my life.

On the express desire of the superior, and in order to honor the memory of the Foundress of the Lisieux Carmel, who died December 5, 1891, Céline had to change her name from Marie of the Holy Face to Geneviève of Saint Teresa. Sister Thérèse of the Child Jesus, who had given her the first noble title, was a little disturbed by this substitution. Yet she tried nonetheless to console her sister. "Both of us will have the same patroness", she said, referring to the Reformer of Avila. Sister Geneviève replied, not realizing she was being prophetic: "You will be my patroness." With her new name, the novice received the precious relics of the Foundress of the Lisieux Carmel: her belt buckle, her cross, and her rosary medal, as well as a sentence written out by the Foundress that Céline loved to repeat and that she very carefully framed: "I am chained, and yet I am free."

For the moment, she was particularly aware of the weight of her new bonds. Having entered Carmel at twenty-five years of age after having enjoyed, in the world, much attention and complete autonomy in governing her own household, naturally inclined to be independent and incapable of concealing her opinions, she found herself enclosed within the narrow structure of the monastery, hemmed in by the whole network of observances that often made no sense to her. She was the newcomer, that is to say, subject to everyone and called upon to help everyone, without ever assuming personal responsibilities. Because of her many talents, she was asked to give all kinds of nonessential services. For a certain feast of the Mother Prioress, she had to decorate about forty small articles, a task she willingly discharged. In the world, she, along with her cousin Marie Guérin, had had a passion for photography and had even taken part in an exhibition of amateurs. With the consent of Mother Agnes of Jesus, she brought her equipment to Carmel: a 13 x 18 camera, Darlot lens, and all the paraphernalia that went with it. She worked like a virtuoso in filling the community album and in providing much-appreciated mementoes for the sisters' families and for fellow monasteries. We can thank the Lisieux superiors for their liberalism in this matter, since any art thought to be frivolous was considered to be an infringement of the rules then in force and, in the name of the spirit of enclosure, was banned from most monasteries. Céline was responsible for most of the plates found in the album *Visage de Thérèse de Lisieux*.

Sister Geneviève had to keep busy in order to get everything done. She had, moreover, a remarkable ability in executing her work quickly while at the same time giving extreme attention to detail: all had be done to perfection. This earned her more than one reproach: she was not detached enough from her work; she displayed some irritability about it; she did not stop what she was doing at the first sound of the bell; she did not put up with interruptions very well. Now it happened that one old sister thought it her duty to exercise her unseasonably, while another, afflicted with cerebral anemia, called her frequently for no reason at all until one day she told Céline that she needed to watch her step and try to be like her sister. Céline exploded but immediately regretted it. The whole thing wounded her deeply, because, as she noted, "It is true, as one wise man put it, that you feel a pinprick on yourself more than the broken arm of your neighbor."

There was more. These series of incidents made her lose any illusions she had about herself. Painfully, she began to examine her weakness. She writes with beautiful clarity:

> In the world, my soul lived, so to speak, in a strong fortress: it was quartered there and reveled in its riches. On the inside as on the outside, everything obeyed it. Praised and applauded, it had no doubt that it was really something. Moreover, did it need to be praised from without when it felt itself so alive with constantly renewed energy, when the good God set before it, so to speak, the gifts that he had so liberally accorded it?
>
> But suddenly the picture changed. In place of the edifice, I no longer saw anything but ruins that allowed the hitherto ignored chasms to be discovered. Then war was enkindled in me: my faults, which up till then had been slumbering, were awakened. Was it to live with them that I had come to Carmel?

In the novitiate with Céline were two lay sisters,[1] Sisters

[1] The lay sisters of a religious community do not have the obligation of saying or singing the Divine Office in choir. They are thus freed to perform some of the necessary tasks, such as cleaning or cooking.

Martha of Jesus and Marie-Madeleine of the Blessed Sacrament, and one choir sister, Marie of the Trinity; her cousin, Marie Guérin, came eleven months later to join the little band. This group, through the exchanges it gave rise to, provided an opportunity for the lively spirit, emulation, and fraternal charity it permitted. However, it was no less an occasion for tension and minor friction. Sister Geneviève wrote later,

Admittedly, we were surprised that religious had to practice such struggles against nature. I confess that I myself shared that astonishment at the beginning of my Carmelite life. It seemed to me that after having made the sacrifice of separation from one's family and of renouncing the whole world, it ought to be easy to put up with the thousand little clashes of community life. I was very quickly set straight, and by personal experience.

In the cloister there is no such thing as the hundreds of diversions that serve to distract an injured sensibility. The latter therefore experiences much more keenly the little misunderstandings inevitably provoked by different temperaments, education, and characters. One therefore sees souls who are heroic in the face of great sacrifices having to put up a bitter struggle when it comes to minor incidents. This is what Sister Thérèse pointed out to me.

These were minor dramas that scarcely disturb those who have some experience with the beginnings of religious life. When Sister Geneviève complained, Mother Agnes of Jesus answered in a matter-of-fact tone of voice: "Are you finding it too hard? Do more." And the novice, taking the words literally, reacted with all her strength.

Nevertheless, she suffered because she could no longer receive Holy Communion every day, since the community followed the regulations then in force of communicating three or four times a week. On February 3, 1895, she gave herself completely into the hands of the Blessed Virgin. "You are the

Mistress of my house", she loved to tell her. As special protectors, she chose Saint John the Baptist, who humbly effaced himself before Christ; Elias, intrepid zealot for the glory of God; and Saint Michael, destroyer of Satan in the name of the sovereign power of the Most High God.

II. Her Noviceship under the Direction of a Saint

In order to overcome the obstacles along the way, the beginner had the advantage of having at her side a saint who was her own sister. In her autobiography, Thérèse herself declares with regard to Céline: "I can say that my sisterly affection was more like the love of a mother; I was filled with dedication and solicitude for her soul." Shortly before her death, on July 16, 1897, in alluding to Father Pichon's desire to draw Céline to Canada, she confided to Mother Agnes of Jesus:

> I had made the complete sacrifice of Sister Geneviève, but I cannot say that I desired it. Very often in the summer during the hour of silence before Matins, when I was seated on the balcony, I said to myself: "Ah! if only my Céline were here near me! . . . But no, this would be too much happiness." And that seemed to be an unrealizable dream to me. Yet, it was not merely natural affection that made me desire this happiness; it was for her soul, so that she might follow my little way. And when I saw her enter here—and not only enter, but given to me completely to instruct—when I saw how God exceeded my desires, I understood the immensity of his love for me.

After February 20, 1893, Thérèse served as assistant to the mistress of novices, Mother Marie de Gonzague. When the latter succeeded Mother Agnes of Jesus as prioress, she fulfilled that office simultaneously with that of novice mistress but kept her young assistant at her side. This is how Thérèse was led to play a decisive role in Céline's formation. Her religious spirit, always developing, had then almost reached its full maturity through a whole series of experiences and investigations. Holy Scripture, confirming all her intuitions, gave her the key to what would one day be called "spiritual childhood" and which she herself called the "little way", or the "way of love and confidence". An interior inspiration urged her to communicate the grace that dwelled within her and that transported her irresistibly to the summits of divine union.

This was more than a joy for her; it was a real stroke of luck to find in Céline the ideal disciple, so receptive, open, spontaneous, sympathetic, and at the same time a person with her own opinions, curious, rational, and capable of reacting. By her requests for explanations, her resistance, even her objections, the pupil would force the mistress to examine her message thoroughly, to present it concretely, to rethink it, and to adapt it to the capacity of a youthful fervor not yet exempt from weaknesses and relapses. A soft dough would have recorded passively, without being able to serve as an interpreter or as proof. A vigorous and not in the least conformist temperament would offer future generations consequential testimony at the same time as it would stimulate in Thérèse what one would dare to call the perfection and the pedagogy of her spiritual doctrine. In this sense, was it not providential, though somewhat unusual, that a fourth member of the Martin family was admitted into a community whose Rule limited the number of subjects?

As for Sister Geneviève, the roles between her and Thérèse had long been reversed, and although she was the elder, she placed herself under the direction of her younger sister. "I always come after you", she wrote to her on March 1, 1889: "I am another you; but you, you are the reality, while I am only your shadow." Henceforth, she would benefit from this

"Sometimes we also had deep, intimate conversations." Céline and Thérèse were meeting again . . . and talked of the mysteries of the future life, of predestination, of the rewards of suffering, of martyrdom.

contact, whose law she sketched one day: "Just as a sponge full of water cannot be touched without its communicating the liquid with which it is saturated, so one cannot draw near to a saint who exudes divine grace from all his pores without feeling his influence. This is why saints are so useful to the Church."

When she was asked if, on her arrival in the cloister, she noticed anything extraordinary about Thérèse, Sister Geneviève declared: "No, she was not extraordinary, but I was always struck by her answers. The Holy Spirit spoke through her. That is certain." On her part, the young novice mistress appreciated in this chosen disciple the ardent desire of being everything to Jesus, a spirit that persisted right to the end, a basic generosity capable of the greatest sacrifices. Above all, she admired her straightforwardness and her transparent loyalty: "When I think of you in the presence of the one friend of my soul," she had written to her on April 25, 1893, "it is always simplicity that is presented to me as the distinctive characteristic of your heart." She returned to this in a poem dedicated to her sister that is entitled: "The Queen of Heaven to Her Beloved Child Marie of the Holy Face."

> I want sweetness and purity
> To shine on your brow,
> But the virtue that I give you
> Above all is Simplicity.

When Sister Geneviève confided to her the assaults that her chastity had undergone in the world, the Saint took her in her arms and said to her tearfully: "Oh! I am so happy today! . . . How proud I am of my Céline! Yes, today I am again seeing one of my desires realized, for I had always desired to give God that kind of suffering, and my soul was never tried like that, but since it afflicted the soul of my Céline, this other me, then I am fully satisfied: together we will offer to Jesus all kinds of martyrdom."

Thérèse did not hesitate to revive all their past life at Les Buissonnets. It was confidences of this kind, made one evening in December 1894 to her three sisters, that led Mother Agnes of Jesus to ask her to write her childhood memoirs. The Saint occasionally used charming nick-names—a custom inherited from M. Martin—that were prevalent previously in her correspondence with Céline and that will be found in her poetry. With her, they were sweet and sentimental only in appearance, for she hid beneath this naïve covering some strong and salutary lessons. When she speaks in a tender way of "the little shadow", or of the "little lyre of Jesus", of the "Immortal Lily", of the "sweet echo of my soul", or of the "dewdrop", or "dear little Veronica", the intention is always to detach what she sensed to be a tender and loving heart from itself and to fix it on God. In this regard, she showed complete patience and receptivity. Sister Geneviève willingly recalled the day when, having upset an inkwell on the white wall and the floor of her cell, she went in great distress to look for her sister, who, pacifying her with a smile, helped her to repair the damage.

Even in these fraternal relationships, mortification was not lacking. Céline explains it very frankly: "Because she had been given charge of the novices, my communications with my dear Thérèse were very frequent, but even in that I was to encounter the cross. Since I was not the only 'kitten drinking out of the Infant Jesus' bowl', I was not supposed to take more than the others or to go back to it more often but, on the contrary, I was, through my discretion, to try to win forgiveness for the privilege of being her sister. This was the source of great sacrifices for me."

November 1896: from left to right, Sister Marie of the Sacred Heart; Mother Agnes of Jesus; Sister Geneviève (Céline); Sister Marie of the Eucharist (Marie Guérin); Sister Thérèse of the Child Jesus

Nevertheless, the Saint knew how to be firm and exacting. One can surmise this from Sister Geneviève's own admissions.

When my turn came to see her, I was very happy, and in these too short moments, the two sisters would resume the conversations we earlier had begun by the windows on the belvedere. . . . The theme, however, had changed a bit, for the surge of enthusiasm for suffering and scorn were presently being lived; virtue under the guise of flowers and desires had become virtue in action; the petals of my flower had been picked off, and the still-green fruit was being formed in laborious transformations of a painful and hidden work.

As for Thérèse, her fruit was ripe, and the Divine Gardener was getting ready to pluck it, but mine was only just taking shape; there was at that time more of a difference between Thérèse and Céline than before in their early years; the two little sisters were no longer equal. . . . That presupposes more self-sacrifice than joy in the mission my Thérèse fulfilled in my regard. Without seeking personal consolation, she labored hard to do away with the illusions and prejudices I had brought with me from the world, for however impervious one may be by the grace of God, it is still impossible not to retain some vestiges of the world's coloring. I really had been steeped in it too long not to be affected by it. . . . She taught me the art of warfare, pointed out the pitfalls to me, the ways of conquering the enemy, and the manner of bearing arms; she led me step by step into each day's struggles.

Céline was too "self-centered" to have what could be called spontaneous humility, although she always had the desire and love for that virtue and did make substantial progress in it. She demonstrated this on the Pentecost of 1895, when Mother Agnes of Jesus wanted one member of her family to join the lay sisters and chose Céline. She acquiesced without hesitation, and the matter would have been settled if Mother Marie de Gonzague had not opposed it.

This little flicker was nevertheless far from the ideal Thérèse had in mind. She intended to draw her Céline into her little way, to have her go down into the valley from which she aspired to ascend, and to forbid any association between "worth" and "profit". Such a conversion could not be accomplished straightaway.

Sister Geneviève gives us some interesting details on the manner in which her sister guided those souls entrusted to her—whether through passing conversations or daily observations, in the regular private discussions, or even in group conferences of the novitiate—from the moment Mother Marie de Gonzague left this matter entirely to her, since she was so absorbed by the responsibilities of her office as superior.

Each day after Vespers, from two-thirty to three o'clock, she assembled the novices. She did not give them a conference properly speaking. There was nothing systematic about her teaching. She read or had them read a few passages from the Rule, the Constitutions, or the Customs Book, which they jokingly called "the Extortion Bill", and gave them explanations or clarifications she felt useful; or she answered questions asked by the young sisters and then corrected their shortcomings when necessary and spoke informally with them about things that were of interest to them at the moment, from spiritual matters even to the work they were doing. In her private conversations with the novices, the Saint gave advice especially adapted to each one. She shed light on the matters of conscience and the difficulties of her novices according to their personal tendencies, their peculiar needs, and their current trials and joys.

Céline showed a touch of pride in stressing her victories and excusing her failures. Thérèse firmly tore aside the deceptive veil:

You must never believe, when you don't practice virtue, that it is due to some natural cause like illness, time, or grief. You must draw a great lesson in humility from it and take your place among the little souls, since you are able to practice virtue only in such a feeble manner. What is necessary for you now is not to practice heroic virtues but to acquire humility. For that, your victories must of necessity always be mixed with failures, so that you cannot take any pleasure in thinking about them.

Sister Geneviève envied the good memory that enabled the Saint to retain literally many passages from Scripture; Thérèse quickly found fault with her: "Ah! there you go, wanting to own wealth, to have possessions! To rely on that is to lean on a red-hot iron! It leaves a little mark! You must not rely on anything, even on what can help piety." She taught her to surrender all things blindly to "God's bank".

"One time," declared Céline laughingly, "I had to give her my hand, and she wrote in ink on my fingernail: 'Love of riches', and made me keep this mark on for quite some time."

The natural overeagerness and feverish application of the young novice to the duties assigned her were mercilessly noticed, exposed, and restrained.

You devote too much of yourself to what you are doing, as if each thing were your final goal, and you never cease hoping to reach it; you are surprised when you fall. You must always expect to fall. You worry about the future as if you were the one responsible for it; but then, I understand your anxiety. You are forever saying to yourself: "O my God, how is this going to pass from my hands!" Everybody looks for success like this; it's the ordinary way. The only ones who do not look for it are the poor in spirit.

A person cannot raise herself to such heights immediately. More than once Céline met with difficulties. "It is impossible; I cannot rise above them!"

"Go underneath", Thérèse replied, referring to a humorous incident from their childhood at Alençon: a horse barred access to the garden; the women made a detour around it, but the little girls nimbly slid "underneath" the animal and happily attained their end. "That is what one gains by being little. There are no obstacles for little ones. They slip through everywhere."

Saint John of the Cross was just as resolute in driving out the calculations of self-love as was Francis of Assisi in denouncing the proprietary instinct. The dialectic of the *todo* and the *nada* was no secret to Thérèse. She, too, made one aware of the "nothing" of the creature in order to make one's way toward the "all" of God.

Céline was attached to a pin that she thought perfectly suited for a particular purpose and regretted having lost it. "Oh! how rich you are!" Thérèse reproached her. "You cannot be happy!"

Once, the novice gathered some snowdrops without permission. It had to be pointed out to her that the garden in Carmel was not that of Les Buissonnets, where she was "mistress". In her suffering, she turned to God, her only refuge, and consoled herself by trying to improvise a hymn, for which she could come up with only the two first lines:

> The flower I pluck, O my King,
> Is you.

Thérèse took the idea and developed it into stanzas that restored peace to the contrite soul. She wrote nothing lovelier. This "Canticle of Céline" was later published under the title: "*Ce que j'aimais* [What I loved]".

Another time, it was Sister Geneviève who asked the Saint to put into verse all the sacrifices she was aware of having offered to Jesus. The answer came swiftly, as if by return mail, but considerably modified. It is the poem: "*Jésus mon Bien-Aimé, rappelle-toi* ["Jesus, My Beloved, Remember!"]", which enumerates the sacrifices consented to by Jesus in order to attach himself to Céline. The shift in subject and its educational importance are clear.

Thérèse used all her skill in leading her sister to recognize, to accept, and to cherish her misery, seeing in it a justification for arousing merciful love and for drawing upon its munificence.

> She was happy [wrote Sister Geneviève] to see me struggle step by step with the faults that constantly kept me in a state of humiliation, for, with my impulsive temperament, I often had little outbursts with the sisters that afflicted me a great deal on account of my self-love. I thought my exterior was deceiving, that I was better than I appeared to be: from that, I developed a certain frustration at not being judged at my true worth. . . . Then my little sister endeavored, by her penetrating instruction embellished with symbolic stories adapted to my circumstances, to make me love the shame I was in. She told me "that if there had been no imperfection in falling, it would be necessary to make it so in order to be exercised in humility." She made me find my joy in believing that I was a "very little soul" whom God constantly had to support because it was nothing but weakness and imperfection. She wished, moreover, that I would come so far as to desire that the others would notice my faults so that they would scorn me and always judge me to be a religious without virtue.

"It is not for you to be a justice of the peace", remarked the Saint cleverly. "Only God has that right. Your mission is to be an Angel of peace." And she exhorted Céline to think of herself as "a little slave whom everyone has a right to command and who would not dream of complaining about it, since she is a slave".

Thérèse's gentleness—the marvelous smile that won her all hearts and that no photograph could ever succeed in capturing, for her soul shone through it all—welcomed the most severe trials submissively. She joined to them her genial talents, whose childlike appearance should not fool us: a poem or a canticle that encased a whole teaching, and that the novice discovered in her sandals on a Christmas morning or on the occasion of an anniversary; a symbolic picture that conjured up the beauties of childhood; a toy that would serve, better than a parable, to call to mind abandonment into the hands of Jesus; even that envelope of December 25, 1896, which bears the simple notation: "From the Blessed Virgin. To my dear child without refuge in this foreign land." There follows a maternal exhortation to understand the price of suffering and interior poverty, with this conclusion, which tempers the appeal for sacrifice: "One day you will come with your Thérèse into beautiful heaven; you will take your place on the knee of my beloved Jesus; and I, too, will take you in my arms and overwhelm you with caresses, for I am your Mother."

One year earlier, the Saint had taken this same perspective on the back of a holy card representing the Infant Jesus cutting lilies. Under the double signature of Céline and Thérèse was written this prayer: "O my God, we ask that your two lilies may never be separated on earth. Together may they console you for the little love that you find in this valley of tears and that, in eternity, their corollas may shine with the same brightness and exude the same perfume when they incline toward you."

Sister Geneviève knew that she was loved by her young mistress with an affection as deep as it was exacting. The Saint later acknowledged that she had suffered because no one had thought to reserve a place for Céline at her side in the group photographs. When the whole community posed before the camera in the laundry room, she could stand it no longer and asked Sister Martha of Jesus to move over a bit so that she might have her lifelong companion near her. The two sisters were so close that even their voices sounded the same; they had the same intonations and the same accent to the point where they were easily taken for each other when they recited the lessons in choir.

Céline was not the only one to profit from this trusting friendship. Thérèse knew how to make the most of it in order to develop her thought, her spiritual sayings, and her original reflections, and even her pupil's points of inquiry. The latter made her a gift of some collections of Scripture quotations that she had put together for herself in the world. The Saint later drew from them several of the texts that would serve to support her "little doctrine". She herself offered her sister a holy picture that had, on one side, photographs of four young brothers and sisters turning toward God; on the other side were verses from the Gospels, from the prophet Isaiah, and from Saint Paul extolling spiritual childhood and the free gift of justification.

At the heart of such sisterly affection a passionate love for Jesus shone out resplendently. On this subject, Thérèse one day posed this question point-blank to her sister: "Do you prefer to say to him 'thee' [*tu*] or 'you' [*vous*] when you pray?" "I answered", Céline confides, "that I preferred to say 'thee'." Quite relieved, Thérèse answered, "So do I; I much prefer to say 'thee' to Jesus; that expresses my love better, and I always use it when I speak to him alone; but in my poems and the prayers that are to be read by others, I do not dare."

Moreover, it was Sister Geneviève who surprised the Saint by covering her crucifix with roses and making the gesture of removing the nails and the crown of thorns from Christ. It was she who, seeing her in her cell while she was sewing, was struck by her expression of intense recollection: "What are you thinking about?" she asked her.

"I am meditating on the 'Our Father'. It is so sweet to call God our Father! . . ."

In such a remarkable atmosphere, asceticism, as severe as it was, did not run the risk of being gloomy or frightened. It was radiant and as if sunny. Thérèse urged her pupil to attach herself to Jesus in an ongoing movement of absolute trust, pleasing him in everything, even the smallest things, and neglecting none of those little attentions through which love is expressed. "At times", Céline confesses, "I would go to her so discouraged, feeling that I could no longer continue, finding myself so imperfect all along the line. She received me with such kindness, and listened to me so well, that I would go back ready to pursue the battle." Jesus always had the last word.

III. Her Profession and Veiling

This effort bore fruit. Sister Geneviève was not stripped of all her faults, but she learned to use them in order to get in touch with her poverty. To help her in this, Thérèse made her a partner from the very first in a step that marked an important turning point in her spiritual life. Here again, we have Céline's own words to tell us about it. Her direct witness is of more value than any commentary.

It was June 9, 1895, during Mass on the Feast of the Holy Trinity, when my little Thérèse was inspired to offer herself to the Merciful Love of God. Already, three months before, during her hour of adoration at the Forty Hours Devotions on Tuesday, February 26, she had composed in one sitting her canticle: "Vivre d'Amour" ["Living on Love"] according to her personal inspirations. On Trinity Sunday, then, she was inspired to offer herself as a victim to Merciful Love. Right after Mass, very much moved, she dragged me off after her; I did not know why. But soon we caught up with Mother Agnes of Jesus, who was taking her mail to the Turn. Thérèse appeared a little embarrassed to make her request known. She stammered a few words, asking for permission to offer herself with me to Merciful Love. I do not know if she uttered the word "Victim". The thing didn't seem important. Our Mother said "yes".

"Once we were alone, she explained to me a little of what she wanted to do; she was very moved; she had a flushed look. She told me that she was going to put her thoughts into writing and compose her offering. Two days later, kneeling together before the Miraculous Virgin, she pronounced the Act for both of us. It was June 11.

Among the memorable dates in her life, Sister Geneviève noted one that followed shortly after this event: September 8, 1895. She records there an indescribable grace that she summarized in this way: "Jesus living in Céline; Céline possessed by Jesus."

The hour of her profession was drawing near. Marie Guérin had entered the Carmel on August 15, 1895; she was supposed to receive the habit before long; there was a question of combining the two ceremonies. In the light of her oblation, Céline, who loved to think of Jesus as her Knight, did a pen-and-ink drawing of his coat of arms and annotated it on a sheet of paper dated November 1, 1895. There she expressed the meaning of her vocation, which she had summarized in her response to the question in the canonical examination: "What drew you to Carmel?": "Since Jesus wanted to give his life for me, I wanted to give mine to him." Later, she had a strong desire to destroy this paper, judging it to be "counterfeit money", as Thérèse said, that is, beautiful declarations not put into practice. Her sister, however, dissuaded her, and she herself composed for her, on parchment paper, using the same theme, a true coat of arms with a marriage contract between Céline and Jesus, all placed in an envelope with a wax seal. There still had to be a motto. Questioned on this point, Sister Geneviève answered rashly, thinking of one of her childhood games: "The one who loses wins!" Quick to turn everything to account, the Saint recorded at that moment, in spite of the protestations of her sister, these words that to her took on a more evangelical ring: "To leave oneself in order to find God." The missive was marked "From the Garden of Agony" because it was in commemoration of that mystery, on February 24, 1896, that Sister Geneviève made her profession. On the day before her profession, the document was deposited in the novice's cell with the following address: "From the Knight Jesus to my beloved spouse, Geneviève of Saint Teresa, living by love on the Mountain of Carmel."

The date for the ceremony had not been set without difficulty. Mother Marie de Gonzague, mistress of novices, wanted to delay it. Actually, new elections were soon to take place, and she herself wanted to preside at the ceremony. It is on this occasion that Thérèse observed: "That is not on the list of humiliations that can be inflicted." Mother Agnes of Jesus consulted the Bishop's representative, and he was opposed to any delay.

Two days before the great day, Sister Geneviève was prey to alarming attacks in which she doubted her vocation and felt as if she were acting a farce. In prayer, everything was made calm again. Comforted by the papal blessing of Leo XIII, which the faithful Brother Simeon[2] had obtained for her, she made her vows in the hands of her sister Pauline, "Little Mother" of the whole family. She carried over her heart a

[2] Brother Simeon, who was in his eighties at the time, was in Rome, and on various occasions he obtained papal blessings for the Sisters.

prayer wherein she had summarized all her aspirations. It read, in particular: "Lord, my ambition is to be, with my dear Thérèse, a little child in the Father's heavenly home. . . . I desire only to work for your pleasure. . . . I agree always to lose here below, for I want everything I receive from you to be gratuitous, because you love me and not the riches acquired by my virtues. . . . Do not judge me according to my works, do not lay my faults to my charge, but look on the Face of my Jesus. He will answer for me."

On the evening of the celebration, according to custom, they sang to the newly professed a canticle composed in her honor. It was the work of Sister Marie of the Angels. Thérèse, who had wanted to do it, took fraternal revenge when she wrote the verses a year later for the song intended for Marie Guérin. She gave it this title: "*Mes Armes* [My weapons]"; she explored the depths of the chivalric ideas that enraptured Céline, and she said to the latter: "This is what I wanted to offer you; consider it, then, as done for you." At the time, the Saint had given her in compensation a poem in which a delicate reminder of the grace of September 8, 1895, figured; and in addition presented her with an invaluable relic: "The last tear of Mother Geneviève of Saint Teresa". Finally, responding to her desire, she composed for her an "Allegorical Description: The wedding feast of Jesus and Céline in heaven". In simple descriptions, but with depth of purpose, the entire court of the elect is conjured up at length, particularly the deceased members of the Martin family, who incline lovingly toward the spouse of Christ.

The veiling was set for March 17, 1896. Sister Geneviève later rejoiced at discovering that on that same day the Roman Martyrology celebrates the commemoration of Joseph of Arimathea, donor of the Holy Sepulchre. Msgr. Hugonin presided. The sermon was again delivered by Canon Ducellier, who, abandoning the subject suggested by Thérèse, commented on the verse: *Placebo Domino in regione vivorum.* This text, used in the Office of the Dead, was not inappropriate for a ceremony that consecrates that mystical death constituted by definitive separation from the world. In the afternoon, before a packed congregation, Marie Guérin received the Carmelite habit under the name of Sister Marie of the Eucharist. It was on this day that Céline and her Benjamin[3] were photographed side by side near the cross in the inner courtyard.

Mother Marie de Gonzague resumed the office of prioress at the elections of March 21, 1896. While she was in office, there would for a time be a question of sending to Indochina Thérèse herself, then Mother Agnes of Jesus, and finally Sister Geneviève and Sister Marie of the Trinity. The project did not materialize, but it did stimulate the generosity and the spirit of sacrifice in the interested parties. It was in the course of this triennium that the Saint's very short life came brilliantly to its end. The superior, who highly esteemed her and who had the merit of favoring her entrance to the cloister as well as that of her sister and her cousin, gave Céline to her as second infirmarian. Sensing that her end was near, the invalid said compassionately: "Oh! it is my little Sister Geneviève who is going to feel my departure most; certainly, she is the one I pity the most because as soon as she has any difficulty, she looks for me, and she won't have anyone any more. . . . Yes, but God will give her strength . . . and then, I shall return."

On May 13, 1897, when her sister observed the anniversary of her first Holy Communion, Thérèse addressed these lines to her: "Jesus is happy with little Céline, to whom he gave himself for the first time seventeen years ago. He is prouder of what he does in her soul, of her littleness and her poverty,

[3] Thérèse was affectionately called the family's Benjamin because she was the youngest (see Gen 35:15–18; 42:1–4; 43; 44).

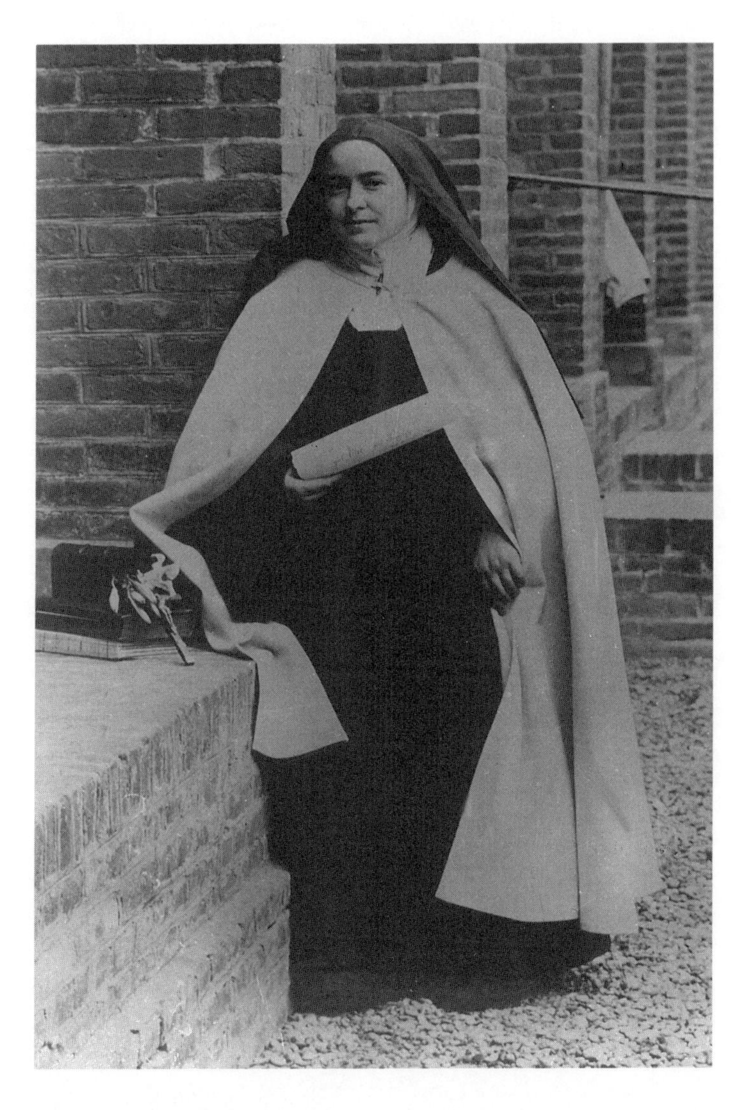

Sister Geneviève of the Holy Face

than he is of the millions of stars he created and the expanse of the heavens."

On Mother Marie de Gonzague's feast day, June 21, the sisters wanted to give her a picture of the sick Thérèse. On June 7, in the sacristy courtyard, Thérèse, mastering her physical exhaustion, posed for Sister Geneviève, who developed the plates immediately in an adjoining cellar. Not quite satisfied with the first two negatives, Céline proceeded to a third sitting, which gave us the impressive image of a Thérèse with a "grand look", as the novices said: serious, strong, taut in the suffering she was mastering.

On the same day, the Saint still found the strength to write to Céline, who had admired her patience and expressed her regret at not being able to imitate her:

> Beloved little sister, let us never seek what appears to be great in the eyes of creatures. . . . The only thing that is not envied is the last place; it is only there in that last place where one finds no vanity or spiritual affliction. However, "the way of man is not for him to decide", and at times, we catch ourselves desiring things that glitter. Then let us humbly rank ourselves among the imperfect and esteem ourselves little souls whom the good God sustains at each moment. As soon as he sees us convinced of our nothingness, he extends his hand to us.

The least incidents and the least conversations were made to refer to this fundamental doctrine. On July 3, in order to dissipate the sadness that enveloped her, Thérèse said to her sister: "I need some nourishment for my soul; read me the life of some saint."

"Do you want the life of Saint Francis of Assisi?" answered Céline. "It will distract you when it speaks about the little birds."

"No, not to distract me, but to show me examples of humility."

IV. At the Bedside of the Sick Thérèse

On Thursday, July 8, Thérèse left her cell for good and was taken down to the infirmary. Sister Geneviève, installed in an adjoining room, watched over her more than ever and left her only to attend Office and to care for the other sick sisters. She was thus a privileged witness of that long agony, which would betoken at the same time the crescendo of suffering and total abandonment.

Brother Leo of Assisi was distressed at seeing the soul of the Stigmatist of Alverno ascend, leaving him farther and farther behind from the one who was both his guide and his father. In the same manner, Céline at certain times gave way to melancholy. But, less timid than "the little lamb of God", she opened up to her sister: "Do you think I can ever hope to be near you in heaven? It seems impossible to me; it is like a little one-armed person trying to catch something high up on a slippery pole." The Saint replied with a smile: "Yes, but what if there's a giant who takes the little one-armed person on his arm, raises her very high and gives her the desired object? . . . That is what God will do with you, but you must not worry about it, you must say to God: 'I know I will never be worthy of what I hope for, but I take your hand like a little beggar and I am sure that you will grant me my wish fully, because you are so good.' "

Sister Geneviève faithfully recorded this new version of "the lift" in order to make it the basis of her spirituality. With still greater emotion, she read the last written message addressed to her by Thérèse: these few sentences that the Saint, on August 3, in a moment of great anxiety, had written for her in pencil on a poor piece of paper: "O my God, how sweet you are to the little victim of your merciful Love! Even now, as you join exterior suffering to the trials of my soul, I cannot say: 'The agonies of death have surrounded me', but I do cry out in my gratitude: 'I am going down into the valley of the shadow of death; yet I fear no evil because you, O Lord, are with me.' "

Cheerfulness still had a place at the bedside of the dying nun. She made it her duty to maintain it, even using puns to cheer up her audience. Céline having declared in one of her remarks: "I won't know how to live without her!", Thérèse retorted tit for tat, "So I will bring you two wings."

Another time, she said playfully to Sister Geneviève, who was leaving her for a time to recite the last little hour of the Office: "Go to say *None*, and remember that you are a very little *nonne* [nun], the last of the *nonnes* [nuns]." She tried to cheer her up by introducing into the most serious conversations wording borrowed from the short plays they had formerly enjoyed at Les Buissonnets: "In heaven, you will take a seat beside me." "My dear little lady, I love you very much, and it is very sweet to be cared for by you."

Fearing that her sister was getting cold, Sister Geneviève offered to bring her one of those pieces of serge that were called in the cloister "a little consolation". Thérèse replied gently: "No, you are my little consolation." Up until her agony, she fulfilled her role as assistant novice mistress: "You are very little, remember that; and when one is very little, she does not have lofty thoughts."

She herself, despite her contagious good humor, lived in the "tunnel", subject to a trial of faith. When Céline mentioned the word *heaven*, Thérèse sighed: "Ah! Tell me something about it." Sister Geneviève spoke about it in a candid and picturesque manner. "That's enough", interrupted the Saint with anxiety, plunged even deeper into the implacable night that haunted her but without ever succeeding in shaking her hope.

Céline wrote to Mme. Guérin: "The other day, I was reading to my little invalid a passage on the blessedness of heaven. She interrupted me to say: 'That's not what attracts me.'

" 'What then?' I asked.

" 'Oh! It is love! To love, to be loved, and to return to earth.' "

Another time Sister Geneviève asked the Saint: "You will look down on us from on high, won't you?"

"No, I will come down."

On August 16, Thérèse said to her: "God asked me if I wanted to suffer for you. I answered that I most certainly did. Then, while up to that point I had suffered only on the right side, my left side instantaneously became incredibly painful." From that time on it was called "Céline's side". A little later, the Saint added, as if to herself: "I am suffering for you, and the devil does not want it! He prevents me from taking the least relief, he holds me as if with an iron hand, he increases my pains so that I will despair."

The day before Thérèse's death, Sister Geneviève asked her if she herself ought not to go to Indochina in her place. "No", she replied sharply. "All is accomplished. It is Love alone that counts." When Céline questioned her on what she said to Jesus, the invalid gave this admirable answer: "I don't say anything to him; I love him."

In a moment of calm, the Saint had declared: "My little sisters, do not be sad if, in dying, my final glance rests on one of you and not the other; I do not know what I will do; it will be whatever God wills. If he gives me my choice, this last glance will be for our Mother, since she is my prioress." Céline goes on to tell us about the conclusion of September 30, 1897. "During her agony, only a few moments before she expired, I was cooling her burning lips with a little piece of ice when, at that moment, she raised her eyes to me and looked at me with a prophetic insistence. Her look was filled with tenderness; at the same time it was a supernatural expression of encouragement and promise, as if to say: "Go, go, my Céline! I will be with you." The community gathered around her bed was in a state of suspense at the sight of this imposing scene, but suddenly our dear little Saint lowered her eyes to search out our Mother, who was kneeling at her side, while her look took on again the expression of suffering it had had earlier." A little later, she pronounced her last words: "My God, I love you"; then came the ecstasy; she fell back and breathed her last.

Sister Geneviève noted in her *Conseils et souvenirs:*

She had hardly expired when I felt my heart ready to break with grief and I hurriedly left the infirmary. It seemed to me, in my naïveté, that I would see her in the sky, but the firmament was covered with clouds, and it was raining. Then, leaning against one of the pillars of the cloister arches, I said, sobbing: "If only there were some stars in the heavens!" I had hardly pronounced these words when the sky became serene, the stars shone brilliantly in the firmament, and there were no more clouds! My uncle and aunt Guérin, who were on their way back home with their umbrellas, after having spent the whole time of our dear little sister's agony in our chapel, were very much surprised at this sudden change and asked each other what it could mean.

Céline took two photographs of the deceased. The first one, in the infirmary the day after her death just before the removal of the body, preserved the smiling reflection on the Saint's face. The second one, three days later, when Thérèse lay on view in her flower-bedecked coffin in choir, conferred on her cold features a majestic dignity and something of the grandeur of the hereafter.

Sister Geneviève inherited an even more touching souvenir. Having observed a teardrop form on Thérèse's eyelids, she drew near and gathered up the precious relic on a handkerchief. Then, her heart broken but thoroughly convinced of the glories that would one day be Thérèse's, she understood at once both her loss and her treasure. Two weeks later, a living flame that traced an immense circle in the depths of the night sky seemed to her to be a posthumous manifestation of Thérèse's soul. This phenomenon, accompanied by a very strong interior grace, was experienced with so much certainty that Céline gave witness to it at the Canonical Process.

On March 5, 1898, she experienced a favor of another kind. At the end of her long retreat, she was meditating on this passage from Zechariah: "For what is the good thing of him and what is his beautiful thing, but the corn of the elect, and wine springing forth virgins?" (Zech 9:17). As she affectionately reproached her sister for not helping her during this exercise, she felt enveloped by an inner sweetness accompanied by the warmth of divine Charity.

". . . the most intimate of my desires, the greatest of all, which I thought I would never see realized, was the entrance of my dear Céline into the same Carmel as ours" — Sister Thérèse of the Child Jesus, ms A.81v°

4

In the Wake of Thérèsian Glory

I. With Paintbrush and Pen

Sister Geneviève did not have time to be affected by the deep void left by the death of Thérèse. From beyond the grave, Thérèse continued to initiate her into the way of childhood; she made her penetrate all its secrets. At the same time, she mobilized the talents of the young professed in order to spread her doctrine. Charged with the illustration of *The Story of a Soul*, which appeared in 1898, Céline at first had recourse to the photographs she had taken of the Saint kneeling and holding the pictures of the Child Jesus and the Holy Face, or again the one by the cross with the rosary in her hand.

Exactly what value did these documents have? It is not inopportune to raise this question since it has been posed so many times and not always with the required impartiality and serenity. All the professionals who have ever had in their hands the negatives produced by Céline recognize their quality. She knew how to make admirable use of the rudimentary equipment of the period and the means of developing the negatives she had at her disposal in a makeshift laboratory. The producer of the film *The True Face of Saint Thérèse* expressed his admiration and astonishment in this regard.

Father Francis of Holy Mary, in the introduction where he

presents to the public the album devoted to this same theme, very objectively assessed the value of Sister Geneviève's style as a photographer and the "manner" in which she took the forty-one pictures in which Thérèse figured, either alone or in a group. He writes,

In the style of her time, Céline took pains to compose the groups of the community or the position of the subjects she wanted to take. She utilized all the possibilities that the monastery offered in the way of scenery: the cloister, the cross in the courtyard, the different statues adorning the courtyards and gardens. All the symbols of the Carmelite of her times also figured in her compositions: the hourglass, the freshly cut fleur-de-lis, the rosary being said, holy pictures being held up as a sign, the staff of the good shepherd, the sacred vessels and the various accessories of the sacristy. The photographer likewise took advantage of the casting of "Thérèse as Joan of Arc", in a costume prepared by makeshift means, for a little play: a wig, a breastplate made out of cardboard, and paper lilies attached to the wool habit . . . a helmet, a chain, a pitcher of water (conventional symbols of a prisoner). A cross positioned on the ground completed the scene.

Even though she was really gifted when it came to composition, Céline did not know how to avoid the artificiality of faces turned a certain way and stereotypical gestures. Certain poses of Thérèse on her knees are a bit theatrical. Photographs taken with less studied care and in a natural setting, on the other hand, are perfectly successful: recreation outside in the chestnut walk, in the laundry room, haying in the meadow, and so forth.

If, at times, a stiltedness is added to the formality, no one could blame the photographer. The camera lenses of the era were not very bright, the plates not sensitive enough; certain poses had to be held up to nine seconds. How could anyone remain themselves all that time? The problem troubled the photographers at a time when their art was as yet only a technique of the pose and was used to immobilize flowers, animals, and people, while the impressionistic painter tried to capture the fleeting moment.

The inevitable imperfections resulting from this fact suggested recourse to the art of retouching. Our Carmelite was thus led to examine closely and to correct the details she judged to be defective. She never permitted herself—thanks to her for this!—to tamper with the negatives themselves, which enabled them to be used later on, and even to be restored somewhat by modern techniques.

Besides, Céline felt—and it was then common opinion, even and especially among cultivated people—that photography gave only a rigid image, from which expression was absent. The snapshot was unknown. The portrait alone seemed to her capable of expressing a person in his deepest attitudes. She therefore willingly acceded to the desire of those who wanted her to paint, for the second edition of *The Story of a Soul,* a half-length portrait, or bust, which would be called the "oval" portrait or the "authentic" portrait. Based on the original photographs, it was judged by the Carmel to be a perfect likeness. "It seems that I am seeing her again", exclaimed Sister Marie-Madeleine, Thérèse's novice. The Guérin family was least satisfied, but their testimony, which did have some value, was undoubtedly influenced by the prevailing memory of Thérèse's face in the world. Perhaps, too, there was a certain annoyance experienced in the face of the clamor made in Lisieux by the first miracles attributed to the young nun.

Céline did not have any fixed set-up for her darkroom. As for the painting workshop, containing only the most rudimentary materials, it was situated in the room next to Thérèse's cell until this was made over into the oratory of the Virgin of the Smile. It was then moved to the library, then to the chapter room, and finally into half of Saint Mechtilde's cell. Our artist spent all her free time there when she was not employed in her duties as sacristan. She had to attend to everything—decorations, woodwork, the restoration of statues, creches, medallions, reliquaries, ornaments for all kinds of things, altar linens, hangings for the altar of repose, programs, miniatures and trinkets of every kind, frames, candlesticks, banners, and baskets. Certain unkind remarks were being made about these extracurricular activities, but Mother Marie de Gonzague put a stop to the criticism by taking advantage of the arrival of Bishop Amette, on the occasion of a ceremony honoring Blessed Denis of Honfleur and Blessed Redemptus, both of the Carmelite Order. She introduced to him the one who had produced the beautiful canvas representing the Apotheosis. He overwhelmed her with praise and encouraged her, in front of the whole community, to continue with her art. Among a variety of religious subjects, the pictures and sketches representing Thérèse on her deathbed, Thérèse at ten years of age, Thérèse with her harp, Thérèse and her mother, and Thérèse and her father all date from this period.

Céline was already so excited about her work that she did not lose one minute. The work poured from her hands. She appeared very rarely in the parlor. M. Guérin understood it, calling her humorously "Mr. Minister", and charged Sister Marie of the Sacred Heart with his errands. Before long, at the desire of the Bishop of Bayeux, she was asked to write for the general public, in order to teach them the way of childhood, an *Appeal to Little Souls*, which later became *Appeal to Divine Love*. It is a pamphlet of about thirty pages that sets forth in three parts the short life of Thérèse in the world, the virtues she practiced in the cloister, and finally her sickness and death. It is essentially comprised of quotations from *The Story of a Soul*, judiciously chosen and joined together by a clearly written, unpretentious text; the object was to direct hearts and minds toward the message of the

Servant of God, whose life was but a concrete illustration of it. Paralleling this publication, Céline gathered together her memories of the future Saint. Add to that her personal notes, which were always very abundant, the occasional poems, and needlework, and one can readily understand the reflections of one old sister who said to her naïvely: "If cats did not have eyes, you would make them some."

At certain times, Céline was ready to beg for mercy. "God", she writes, "never allows anything to go smoothly in my life; rather, all is extracted through unrelenting effort. How many times when I was climbing the stairs to the dormitory did I read that sentence written on the wall: 'Today a little work! Tomorrow, eternal rest!' Then, interiorly, I would correct it: 'Much work today! And after a long time, alas! eternal rest!' "

This activity was all the more meritorious since Sister Geneviève followed community observances strictly and was subject to severe interior struggles. In fact, in February 1899, she felt stricken, in mind and imagination, by terrible temptations against chastity. At certain times, she noticed, as it were, a rising in the depths of her being of all the materialist objections. Heaven was closed to her; prayer seemed dry and without consequence. She braced herself; she clung to God with all her will, in total faith. "The only grace I ask of you", she said, "is never to offend you." She gave her resistance an apostolic meaning: "The desire to save souls was like a mania for me," she wrote of this period, "and in comparison to a single soul snatched from Satan, all my difficulties seemed as nothing to me. It was this hope that gave me courage."

This state of soul lasted for two years and three months, with climactic points, especially on the days of April 24 and 25, 1901, when she responded to the bravado from hell: "Jesus will be victorious for me." Happily, she derived much consolation from daily communion, which the Abbé Hodierne, successor to the Abbé Youf, who died around the same time as Thérèse, advocated according to the powers given to community chaplains by Leo XIII and which he used most liberally.

II. The Holy Face

The trial subsided at the time when a new chapter was opening up in Céline's life, a chapter of the most passionate kind. "My spiritual life", she would later say, "can be inscribed between two loves: my Thérèse and the Holy Face." The second was about to experience an unexpected development.

The image of the Holy Face, made popular by the holy man of Tours, M. Dupont, based on Veronica's veil preserved at St. Peter's in Rome, had excited the devotion of the Martin family during the illness of their father. It did not offer, however, that character of nobility that is by instinct demanded of the divine effigy. Marie Guérin did not hide her aversion to it. But then it happened that a few weeks after Thérèse's death, a letter of the king of Italy dated November 10, 1897, authorized the public display of the Holy Shroud of Turin. In March 1898, the precious relic was taken out of its circular lead case. It occasioned many pilgrimages and much publicity. M. Guérin procured the book of M. Vignon, *Le Linceul du Christ* (The shroud of Christ), and passed it on to his niece, Céline, whom he knew appreciated photography.

In the evening in her cell, during the hour of silence, the religious spread out the plates that reproduced in positive the negative form imprinted on the cloth steeped in aromatics. She was speechless with emotion.

"I had done . . . the Holy Face . . . with . . . so much love" — Sister Geneviève during her father's last illness

It was truly my Jesus, just as my heart had sensed him to be. . . . And, looking for the marks of his sufferings, I observed by the wounds the imprint of the cruel crown of thorns. I saw blood coagulated in his hair, then running down in large drops. At the top of his head, to the left, one can sense that the crown must have been torn away with difficulty. This force caused the hair matted with blood to stiffen. The left eye seems to be slightly open, while the right one is swollen. I see that the upper part of the nose is fractured, the right cheek and the nostril puffed up by the blows of those who slapped him in the face; the beard is all covered with blood. . . . Then, no longer able to restrain the sentiments of my heart, I covered that adorable Face with my kisses and bathed it with my tears. And I resolved to paint a Holy Face after the manner of this ideal that I had just glimpsed.

Sister Geneviève could not begin the task until Easter 1904 and at first executed a charcoal drawing. The publishing houses that were contacted pointed out that the reproduction would be imperfect. It would be better to do a grisaille [a painting in tones of gray designed to produce a three-dimensional effect]. She started it around Easter 1905, giving all her free time to it: Sundays, feast days, and the set times of silence. She worked standing up, which was a real penance for her, in front of the life-size picture of the Face of Christ, working assiduously with a magnifying glass to pick up the slightest threads in the texture and the corresponding outlines. She who had such a need for sleep sacrificed the time set aside for rest and was content to curl up in a little mound at the foot of her canvas for the last ten minutes, her head propped up on her handkerchief rolled into a ball, which she called "playing the puppy".

She called on all heaven to help her, each evening placing her brushes and work in front of the Virgin of the Smile and, when she was alone, bringing her picture before the Blessed

Sacrament as if to subject it to its divine rays. She shared it also with Saint Joseph as well as all the heavenly court and her own family on high. When the work became too hard, she thought about the sorrowful Virgin on the summit of Calvary. In the course of several months, three or four times—whether it was the effect of a heightened imagination dwelling on the subject or really a choice privilege as reward for her labor—she perceived before her, for the space of a minute ("it was not through bodily eyes", she stated) "the face of the suffering Jesus strikingly beautiful and pure".

When the work was completed, she took it to the Blessed Virgin "in order to offer her the first fruits". She was then inspired to consult the Gospels and came across this verse from Saint Matthew: "All those who were there and who saw what took place said: 'Truly, this is the Son of God.' "

It was, indeed, an authentic masterpiece, which, in March 1909, was awarded the grand prize at the International Exposition of Religious Art at Bois-le-Duc, in Holland. The likeness, of unquestionable majesty in its tragic realism, was popularized by millions and millions of copies. When Pius X saw it, he contemplated it for a long time, murmuring repeatedly: "How beautiful it is!" He added, with his customary kindness: "I want to give a remembrance to the little sister who did that", and he sent to her a large bronze medal with his picture engraved in relief. She appreciated this more, need it be said, than if she had been admitted to the Salon.

Bearing in mind her father's trial, whose memory haunted her in the course of her work, Céline cried out: "Ah! I am not surprised at having succeeded with the sorrowful Face of my Jesus. I know it is said that only a pure soul could have the gift for reproducing so beautiful a Countenance; but I still say that, in order to understand such wounds, a soul would have had to bear its imprints."

Sister Geneviève then painted, after the manner of Saint Suaire and having recourse to the most authentic historical interpretations, Christ at the Pillar and Christ Crucified. Her notes, permeated with ardent conviction, returned frequently to this theme of the Savior's Passion and the establishment of his reign on the Cross. She even went so far as to compose a draft for an Office and Mass in honor of the Holy Face.

Céline always kept this devotion religiously. On November 14, 1916, Mother Agnes of Jesus, then prioress, granted her permission to add to her name the title of the Holy Face. Henceforth, she signed her name, reversing the order of the titles: "Geneviève of the Holy Face and of Saint Teresa." She chose the Transfiguration as her feast day, since she loved to celebrate the resplendent Face of glory in contrast to the suffering Countenance. She painted a banner of the Holy Face, which she herself carried each year in a community procession. Her soul was as if wounded by this loving fervor, and she drew from it an infrangible faith. "Having had in my possession", she writes, "the Face of God, how could I not present myself with assurance before that Face of God? Yes, since the Face of my Jesus is God made visible to me under the appearance of flesh, 'the bow of the mighty is broken, and the feeble have girded themselves with strength' (1 Sam 2:4)."

III. The Love of Christ and His Mother

One can perceive in these lines the passionate tenderness that Sister Geneviève had vowed for Christ. "God has seduced me", she often repeated. "God seized me and conquered me" (cf. Jer 20:7). In her last days, when the world was talking about the Soviets' astronautic achievements, she wrote: "My devotion to the Holy Face is the summary of my devotion to the Sacred Humanity of Jesus. I am the little satellite of his Humanity." Literally, all her religious life she had "circled around Christ". One of her first poems on the anniversary of her profession speaks of him as her "Divine Model". The one she composed for her fiftieth anniversary takes up the theme: To die while living for Jesus, my Spouse.

On Ascension Thursday 1922, commenting on the hymn for Vespers: "*Jesu voluptus cordium*", she was carried away in thought to all the places where the feet of the Savior had walked.

I search, and I look, and I again return
To the familiar scenes for which I yearn,
Wherein the Sacred Humanity by God was placed;
For I know I can find him there ineffably traced.

Then she meditated on Carmel as the New Palestine, frequented by the Divine Presence, and she proclaimed it in verses reminiscent of Lamartine:

O cloisters, O gardens! Earth forever blest!
You pulsate with harmony at my heart's behest.
And you, star of evening, moon of silver disk,
That my only Love looks at so often—and is his,
At my window in the night I can see you high and clear,
And thrill to know his eyes are watching you appear;
At the hour when prolonging his prayer so sublime
He asks for us, his children, a pardon e'er divine.

Sister Geneviève was not satisfied with romantic impressions. The historic Christ was for her the central point of interest. At a time when exegesis was a closed science, she forced open the doors to the cenacle. "All my work", she wrote, "has never stopped me from studying in depth everything that concerns the memory of our Jesus on earth. I have scrutinized the places in Palestine where he passed through. It seems to me that I know the Holy Land as well as if I had lived there." She made collections of scenes from Judea and Galilee; she organized four series of slides on the life of Christ in order to show them to the community. Her commentaries testified to her real scholarly ability.

With her usual attention to detail, she developed for her own use a map of Jerusalem, an outline of the route of the Passion, a diary and a detailed horarium of the events of Holy Week. She gave Mother Agnes of Jesus, for her feast day, a little chest in which she had collected a sample of the twelve stones that, in the Apocalypse, form the walls of the heavenly Jerusalem. Adding to her memories of the Holy House of Loreto details gleaned from creditable authors, with a great deal of ingenuity, she made a reproduction of the house of Nazareth as it must have been in the time of the Holy Family.

Holy Scripture was, above all, her field of her inquiry.

> I could never say [she notes] what it means to me. It seems that if I should live to the end of time I would not need any other book to guide me and instruct me, for I would never exhaust it. I experienced the truth of this when, after having meditated on a passage and examining each word thoroughly—and thinking I had, like the diligent bee, gathered up all the honey enclosed in the many calyces of that mysterious flower—I happened to discover still other horizons and other beauties in it, and I could not understand how they had escaped me.

In the evening of her life, she was delighted to have at her disposal not just a few series of Scripture texts, such as Thérèse was familiar with, but several complete Bibles, old and new. She was intrigued by certain divergences of form and even meaning. "I notice that each author translates according to the idea he has of God. I am very much interested in making a study of these nuances; and I share the same desire Thérèse had to know Hebrew, Greek, and Aramaic in order to translate the original texts according to how my heart perceives the true character of God." She did not hesitate to consult a Scripture exegete in order to probe the inner meaning of any verse in question.

In June 1917, the *Petite somme théologique* (Little theological Summa) of Saint Thomas fell into her hands. She harvested from it some ten pages of quotations about Christ.

> All that the holy Doctor teaches [she wrote in her prefatory remarks] expresses my own thoughts so well that it seems to me that I have learned nothing new as far as the essence of the matter is concerned. But I have seen what I am lacking when I speak of our Lord, and that is the art of proper expression. Thus, I humbly beg that others may not charge me with any involuntary errors I may have committed in all that I have written and may correct those pages if they do not choose to burn them. I repeat here: I do not believe and do not wish to believe anything except what holy Mother Church believes and teaches.

Up to the end, Céline's attention would be focused on the problems involved with the different ways of knowing Christ. In the face of such an effort, one can only regret that she was not given the opportunity to receive a systematic exegetical and theological education. Such a regret is admittedly anachronistic, for in her day, no one had such concerns. Her self-directed research nevertheless supplied her with a wealth of material.

We must add that with Céline, study spontaneously turned to prayer. She approached it with complete faith, mixing prayer and reflection, begging the Holy Spirit to enlighten her, happy with the least light she received and content in her abandonment when the mystery deepened. One can say only that she was a contemplative in the sense, dear to Saint John of the Cross, of the encounter in darkness. There is no doubt that she had, for all that, an overly inquisitive and rational mind. But her ceaseless meditation on the Scriptures placed her, where Christ was concerned, in a state of profound union from which sprang discoveries that filled her notebooks. She lived in the presence of Jesus. At the least infidelity, she was painfully aware of his silence. "Everything is recorded in the heart", she admitted. "Oh! one must never allow oneself to be distracted from this unique vocation!" He was her passion, her obsession. She took great pleasure in looking upon him as a Knight, while she was his lady. "Put me under lock and key, O my Beloved," she told him, "because I am afraid of not being faithful to you." The Canticle of the Furnace, attributed to Saint Francis of Assisi but which served to express his soul in the manner perfected by Jacopone de Todi, moved Céline. When important anniversaries were celebrated, the sisters sang to her or played on the organ the melodic phrase "O Christ, you have enraptured my heart."

Each morning [she wrote] when I go to prayer, I can see the dawn rising and I thrill with hope, because I know just as surely as the horizon is tinged with color before me that Jesus, asleep during the night of this life, will also rise and his glory will shine on me. It will no longer be the "pale morning star", brilliant but fleeting, that I will greet in passing. No, Jesus, whom I have loved so much, my God whom I have found in his Sacred Humanity, he, my Sun, will no longer set. He will be my eternal light and my glory . . . and all this will happen soon.

On September 8, 1900—the anniversary of a signal grace—Sister Geneviève committed to paper these lines that already had the appearance of a last will and testament.

O my Jesus, . . . you know that my desire has always been to love you and to make you loved. Since I cannot express a greater love than that which Thérèse lavished on you, my dream is to lavish it on you myself. Together, and on the same day, O Jesus, you accepted us as little Victims of your Merciful Love. I am the first one to have followed her little way. She opened the door, and I dashed in after her. . . . Is the day very distant when I will hear the sound of your voice, when you will clasp me to your Heart, when I will be able to see your Countenance and kiss your sweet Face, when I will be seated eternally beside Thérèse on your lap? O Jesus, may I live for you and die of Love!

In this journey toward Christ, Sister Geneviève relied on the Virgin. The miraculous cure of Thérèse had left its mark on her life. The statue traditionally venerated by the Martin family constituted for her a sort of sacred trust. It is she who took care of the oratory at Carmel and who continued to do so until 1946. Several times, she received remarkable favors from Mary. She wrote on October 9, 1935,

Yesterday evening, during the time of silence, I felt ineffably united to my heavenly Mother; I experienced an indefinable feeling I dare not express. It seemed to me that the Blessed Virgin was here with us, that she was my sister, my friend; there was a familiarity between us, a kind of equality like that of a family. Oh! how pleasant it was! This morning, during Mass, I was still thinking about it, and it was sweet for me to make the comparison between that grace and the Feast of the Motherhood of the Blessed Virgin we celebrate today. This is the third time in my life that my heavenly Mother has visited me at first Vespers of this very consoling solemnity.

Céline had a very personal way of looking upon Mary. She took Thérèse's thoughts on the manner in which our Lady should be presented—as approachable, affable, imitable, living in faith like us—and pushed them to the extreme. Her notes and her letters show her dialoguing and discussing, with a great deal of assurance, with the teachers and writers who insisted unilaterally on the privileges of the Virgin and who ranked her in an order by itself to the point of seeming to cut her off from the rest of humanity. For Céline, the glory of Mary is ours. The whole of mankind is honored in the Immaculate Conception. With regard to the existence of the Mother of God, it progressed at much the same rhythm as that of most of Eve's children: work, prayer, rest, study of Scripture, with no blazing lights or marvels of any kind. That is what makes her close to us and capable of sympathizing with our ills.

Sister Geneviève praised the passages of the *Philosophie du Credo* (Philosophy of the Credo), in which Father Auguste Gratry establishes the life of faith in Mary. She was fascinated by *Mary, the Mother of Jesus* by Franz Michel Willam. On the other hand, she showed no leniency with a certain speaker who made "exclamation points", as Thérèse termed them, resound from the pulpit in Carmel one December 8.

IV. Cause and Triumph of Thérèse

One will have noted, in many places, that Céline took rather original positions and had some very fixed ideas on a certain number of subjects. She would have occasion to manifest this tendency in the part she took in the canonization of Thérèse.

Matters were not going smoothly. The Guérin family, who appreciated the sanctity of medieval saints, were opposed to the introduction of her Cause. Msgr. Lemonnier, Bishop of Bayeux, was reserved. Msgr. de Teil, who would become Vice-Postulator, was not at all hesitant in saying: "The Congregation of Rites no longer wishes to beatify ordinary religious."[1] This simple, transparent life, without anything sensational about it, did not seem to be material that would move ecclesiastical judges. Nevertheless, to the "shower of roses" the crowds responded by popular vote that they wanted their "little Saint Thérèse". It was Mother Marie-Ange of the Child Jesus, who succeeded Mother Agnes of Jesus as prioress at the elections of May 8, 1908, who induced the Bishop, as a gift of her joyful accession, to undertake the initial steps for beatification. She died on November 11, 1909, so that it fell to Mother Agnes, resuming the office she would never again relinquish, to carry the heavy burden of the rising glory of her sister.

On February 10, 1910, the letter of Msgr. Lemonnier concerning the writings of the Servant of God was made public. On August 12, the first of ninety sessions took place in the course of which forty-eight witnesses were questioned. As soon as Rome became acquainted with the dossier and introduced the Cause, the Apostolic Process was opened, which, from April 1915 on, required new depositions.

Thérèse's own sisters were obviously key figures. It was not a trivial task to confront a dense network of questions, to avoid overlapping and repetition, to place in a favorable light the virtues duly catalogued. Held to the strictest secrecy, the interested parties were able neither to enlighten nor to help each other. How did Sister Geneviève acquit herself of her task? A letter that she wrote at the request of Mother Agnes of Jesus on January 10, 1938, gives us some pungent details on this subject. It merits publication, for our heroine is so aptly described here.

[1] Msgr. de Teil was ill-informed on this matter and obviously did not possess the gift of prophecy.

At the second Process, when the judges questioned me as to my motive in wanting my sister canonized, I answered that "it was solely in order to advance the Little Way of Spiritual Childhood that she had taught us."

Then, they took fright, and every time I spoke those words "Little Way", they gave a start, and the Promoter of the Faith, M. Dubosq, said to me: "If you speak of a 'Way', you will defeat the Cause; you know very well that the Cause of Mother Chapuis was abandoned for that reason."

"Too bad!" I answered resolutely. "If it is defeated, it is defeated; but since I have sworn to tell the truth, I must give witness to what I have seen and heard, no matter what happens!"

With regard to the heroicity of her virtues, I stood by my opinions, and I endeavored to place them in their simple and imitable framework. It was all the more difficult to get this accepted since at the first Process—the Informative Process—the members of the Ecclesiastical Tribunal had misgivings about the proposed Cause. These gentlemen, who set up the Tribunal only through condescension, were persuaded that they should find nothing to give credence to, as we were told later by the Vice-Postulator, Msgr. de Teil. But most often, I protested and told them things like this: "That I would not let Sister Thérèse of the Child Jesus be placed in the circle where custom aligned the other saints, that she had practiced only simple and hidden virtues, and that it would be necessary to get used to it. . . ."

I ask myself how I was able to be so firm; I, who, because of my timidity, had once not wanted to go through my exams, certain that I would become flustered and no longer know anything in front of the examiners. It was necessary for God to arm me for battle, because it certainly was one. M. Dubosq told me I wanted to bring my sister down to my level; and thereupon, he related some very witty stories that appeared to condemn me.

Such as they were recorded, Sister Geneviève's depositions, according to the Consultor of the Congregation of Rites, proved to be remarkable among all the others. They were centered on spiritual childhood but tended also to bring out the virtue of fortitude. With respect to this, Céline made this clarification: "I do not mean an 'inflexible stubbornness'. In regard to that fantastic allegation by certain writers, it is enough for us to affirm that Thérèse, from her tenderest years until her death, seemed to us to be, by her sweetness, her discreet composure, her complete self-mastery, her silent and peaceful reserve, a heavenly copy of the Virgin Mary. It was easy to believe that she was 'confirmed in grace', as her confessors themselves declared to us."

The additional work caused by these events took its toll on Céline's health. In 1911, she developed double pulmonary pneumonia; in February 1915, she suffered an attack of laryngitis that affected her vocal cords for a long time. Nevertheless, she was always hard at it. She was the one who assisted on August 10, 1917—one can imagine with what emotion!—at the second exhumation of Thérèse's remains, in the cemetery of Lisieux. Now and then, her consolations were mixed with grief. Several times, she sensed about her penetrating perfumes revealing an invisible presence. This came to her particularly on February 5, 1912, on the anniversary of her clothing and the day when the Diocesan Process was deposited in Rome. This phenomenon was repeated on March 17, 1925, when she commemorated her veiling and when the Apostolic Process was opened.

On August 14, 1921, Benedict XV promulgated the Decree on the Heroicity of the Virtues. In response to the thanks rendered by the Bishops of Bayeux and Lisieux, he offered a panegyric on Thérèse, centering entirely around spiritual childhood presented as "the secret of sanctity, not only for the people of France, but for the faithful throughout the entire world". In a very thorough analysis, supported by Gospel texts and examples of the Carmelite herself, the Pope showed how spiritual childhood is based on humility, confidence, and abandonment. "The more is known of this new heroine of virtue," he concluded, "the greater will be the number of her followers who will give glory to God by practicing the virtues of spiritual childhood. . . . In the concrete case of Sister Thérèse, one should recognize a special desire on the part of God to exalt the merits of spiritual childhood."

Sister Geneviève of the Holy Face uttered a cry of triumph: "I have never", she writes, "experienced such great and deep joy as I did on August 14, 1921, when Pope Benedict XV made his papal announcement, which enthusiastic telegrams told us had extolled 'the little Way of Spiritual Childhood' as well as the heroicity of Thérèse's virtues. That was the victory I had desired without daring to hope that it would be so complete. The beatification and canonization themselves did not bring me as intense a happiness."

In spirit, Céline shared no less in the imposing celebrations that filled the Eternal City on April 29, 1923, and on May 17, 1925. The triduums celebrated at the Carmel and the Lisieux ceremonies whose echo reached her through the cloister walls all made her feel at times as if it were a dream. On November 25, she wrote:

Finding myself in the garden, in the hermitage of the Holy Face, I saw once again the humiliations that had been our lot and that of our dear father: relatives distancing themselves from us, apologizing for being part of our family; friends and acquaintances who said among themselves: "What good was his piety? He bore the weight of his own sacrifices; and the godless sneer, because of him, at the lamentable end of the just." It seemed to me that then God had said to his angels: "Write", and I saw one of them mark something down on the "Debit" side of a ledger. Since then, many years have passed. Would the All-Powerful delay the day of reckoning? At that moment, I raised my eyes, and I noticed on the cross of Carmel's dome the little glittering star. . . . All the celebrations of our Thérèse's canonization were summarized there, and I heard in my heart these words, words pronounced with indescribable fatherly tenderness: "Are you happy?" Then a wave of gratitude swept over me completely, and, with tears in my eyes, I could only say over and over again with love: "O my God!"

V. The Apostle of the Way of Childhood

The day of the canonization was for the posthumous work of Thérèse less a summit than a new lifting of the curtain. Proclaimed Patroness of the Missions on December 14, 1927, by Pius XI, she extended her influence increasingly throughout the entire world. At Lisieux, it was necessary to go through an immense amount of mail, collect souvenirs, take care of the sanctuaries, receive visitors, and spread the Thérèsian message. This was the joint work of the Carmel and of Abbé Germain, whose zeal as director of the pilgrimage fund was as competent as it was indefatigable. Named prioress for life by the Pope on May 31, 1923, Mother Agnes of Jesus faced with ease the overwhelming task before her. Sister Geneviève actively assisted her. She herself held no offices. She had been seated in the Chapter only since 1915, and then upon the intervention of the Superior of the Order. She had been kept out, as Thérèse herself was, in order to avoid having more than two members of the same family in it. However, Céline's competence compelled recognition. She was relieved of all duties except that of photography and devoted herself entirely to the work concerning Thérèse and her message. She took the lead in drafting her biography for children, which appeared under the name of Father Carbonel. It was a very simple book in tone, illustration, and appearance, as required by the public to whom it was addressed, and contained certain unpublished and enjoyable details.

The publication of the *Petit catéchisme de l'Acte d'Offrande* (Little catechism of the Act of Oblation) claimed the attention of Sister Geneviève, who collaborated closely with Mother Agnes of Jesus, for a longer period of time. As the first to have been initiated into this oblation, which gave an entirely new emphasis in the spirituality of the period, she did not intend to allow its profound meaning to be altered. It was necessary, all at the same time, to avoid the dangers of illuminism, preserve in the process its value as total gift, and to afford access to any soul of good will, whatever its weakness might be. It was equally important to place the oblation in its proper perspective within the framework of spiritual childhood, not as a remote crowning achievement and a height reserved to only a few, but as a basic element and main part. The idea of Merciful Love demanded some clarification. The words *victim* and *holocaust* needed interpretation so as not to excite overly lively imaginations and not to frighten the meek; it was necessary to bring these words back to their proper Thérèsian meaning. Conceived in this way, the tract devoted seventeen questions and answers to defining the Act of Oblation in its general significance and its terminology; the fourteen that followed specified the obligations and the hopes of a soul who surrenders itself. Since then, this subject has aroused a tremendous amount of literature in which the learned vie with each other in casting beams of light from dogmatic and mystic theology. This modest pamphlet in which Céline and Pauline gave their best nevertheless retains its value. It continues to guide the simple and the "poor", in the sense of the Beatitudes, along the path marked out by Thérèse.

Intended for the use of these same readers, another treatise appeared: *Petite Voie* (The little way), which, in thirty-one pictures, annotated by as many stanzas, expressed the ascent of the Saint to the summit of perfection and invited the reader to imitate her. While Mother Agnes of Jesus supplied the text, Sister Geneviève, in conjunction with a designer from outside the monastery, was actively occupied with the allegorical compositions. Contemporary taste calls for less ornamentation and prefers authenticity. This publication was nevertheless successful in its day; and it continues to do good for those who are indifferent to art and style and seek inspiration and comfort in pious illustrations. We must say the same about *La Vie en images* (Life in imagery), which related in flowing stanzas accompanied by photographs and pictures the whole Thérèsian journey. Céline, here again, had to make the greatest effort. Undoubtedly, these were lesser works, but they contributed powerfully toward making the Saint of Lisieux known and loved.

In 1918, Sister Geneviève settled down to a more extensive work, which would serve to express Thérèse's spirit and general orientation. It required an exhaustive and, so to speak, experiential knowledge of the soul of the Servant of God, her life, her writings, her doctrine. It was an ambitious undertaking. Céline worked at it relentlessly for several years until she was completely worn out with cataloguing, verifying, copying, classifying, and regrouping lived events, occasional remarks, and quotations borrowed either from the autobiography, from letters or poems, from the *Novissima Verba*, or from her own notes and the testimonies of her fellow sisters. How was she to clear such a forest? What approaches should she take? From what angle should the illumination be planned?

Sister Geneviève found support and guidance in M. Dubosq, a Sulpician priest who was then superior of the major seminary of Bayeux and who functioned as Promotor of the Faith in the Informative and Apostolic Processes for the Thérèsian Cause. On his advice, she abandoned her plan of focusing entirely on the virtue of fortitude and took for her theme the supreme idea of the love of God.

This book was presented as a mosaic of anecdotes and texts and included precise references in the margins. The author limited herself to selecting, introducing, and joining the pieces together in conformity to an overall plan. It was a matter of her keeping to the background in order to allow Thérèse herself to speak. The style was not without its stumbling blocks. History offers many examples of disciples who imperceptibly substitute themselves for the master, picking over his legacy, prompting his thought, and, at the opportune moment, giving to the documents themselves the decisive push. Would Céline, who was so opinionated and headstrong, not give in to the temptation? Did she, by chance, do so unknowingly?

She was fierce in guarding against this, judging that it would be, more than intellectual dishonesty, an unpardonable crime against the mission entrusted to her and against Thérèse. She even preferred to run the risk of a certain irresoluteness in synthesis rather than to do violence to the scattered elements by forcefully imposing her own construction. At most, she permitted herself, here and there, to support some of the proposed theses by slipping in three or four sentences culled from Ruysbroek, Bossuet, or Msgr. Gay. Knowing her ardent temperament, her inquisitive and original mind, and her gift for developing ideas, one can only guess what the voluntary servitude of such self-restraint of the pen must have cost her.

The first edition—it was followed by many others—appeared in 1923 for the beatification under the title: *The*

Spirit of Blessed Thérèse of the Child Jesus according to Her Writings and Witnesses to Her Life. Four chapters totaling 225 pages showed how the love of God had borne fruit in the life of the young Carmelite, how it shone through her virtues and culminated in spiritual childhood, resulting in incomparable fruits of joy, peace, and blessedness. In the course of the work, stress was laid on the main qualities that characterized the little way: humility, confidence, abandonment, simplicity.

A preface by Cardinal Vico, Prefect of the Congregation of Rites, underlined the merit of the work. Let us note particularly:

> I greatly appreciate the serious and methodical form of this work on the spirit of Blessed [Thérèse]. One can logically deduce from it the special characteristic of her interior life, which is the love of God serving as the foundation of her whole edifice of perfection. From that springs a marvelous fruitfulness in an apparently quite ordinary existence. None of those traits that throw one into astonishment, but the most solid virtue, hidden under an exterior of a delightful simplicity. One finds in these pages the same substance as in the Process, where, even in the smallest details, heroism is revealed.

Hardly had it been put on the market when the book was an instant success. Completed by an analytical table of contents that facilitated its use, it became the main source from which writers, teachers, and eulogists drew material, while historians gleaned from it—at least, before the original manuscripts were available—certain qualities until then unknown, and whose lessons pious souls would never grow tired meditating upon. The eminent Abbé of the Sept-Fons Trappists, Dom Chautard, himself the well-known author of *The Soul of the Apostolate*, hoped that *The Spirit* would be printed in pocket size, like the *Imitation of Christ*.

As for Sister Geneviève of the Holy Face, she was not totally satisfied with the work that had literally worn her out.

On her deathbed, she reproached herself for not having insisted enough on humility, which is at the heart of spiritual childhood. It was necessary to reassure her by quoting excerpts from it where this virtue is beautifully in evidence.

She could not devote herself to this extensive labor—and it appeared overwhelming to her—in a leisurely and calm manner. She also had to attend to the classification of the family records. She took special note of the least details of anything that pertained to Thérèse, reassembled and copied those that were given her by Mother Agnes of Jesus and Sister Marie of the Sacred Heart, and kept up a vast correspondence that, joined to her notes and personal papers—often elicited by formal authority—constituted an enormous, dizzying amount of literature. Between times, particularly on the prioress' feast, or in order to capture some personal feeling, she would try her hand at writing verses, which take some liberties, but lack neither inspiration nor a certain delightful style.

She had so many ingenious ideas and so much practical sense that Mother Agnes of Jesus often depended on her in regard to the works that had to be undertaken or overseen: two illustrated albums, put together by order of her sister with useful notations for posterity, enumerated all that she had done in the various spheres of her activity. It is astounding. There was the recovery and preservation of all that appertained to Thérèse and her family; the arrangement and changes made in the Carmel and its chapel; the purchasing and restoring of Les Buissonnets, the pavilion, and the home where she was born in Alençon; the exhibiting of souvenirs in the outer sacristy or in the inner rooms called the "Gloria" and the "Magnificat"; the care for the arrangement of places and furniture; the illustration of books and brochures, sacred vessels, reliquaries, church linens, and liturgical ornaments; the upkeep of the graves as well as maintainance of correspondence with the Central Office. One wonders how Sister Geneviève of the Holy Face had the time, in her strictly cloistered life, to assume so many responsibilities.

With an unbelievable preciseness and determination, she confronted notaries, architects, artists, and contractors. She always had some supporting plan and also some flash of wit. Seeing a design to be used for a flag bracket in the Carmel's chapel, she slew it in one sentence: "It's perfect for men to hang their hats on." She was feared a little because she was so uncompromising, but she seasoned her conversations with so much good humor! Everyone recognized her talent for organization and hard work. In all these tasks of planning and arrangement, she helped Sister Marie-Emmanuel of Saint Joseph, depositary, who was to follow her closely in death and whom she praised in a letter to Léonie, with impartiality and a sense of mutual collaboration, for her prodigious and well-ordered activity united to all the specifically religious virtues.

In 1929, Sister Geneviève was put on the community council, a position she held until her death.

She had not, for all that, abandoned her brushes. The album in which she reported her material productions reveals the same conscientiousness and overflowing zeal. She had only brief, one-hour periods at her disposal, which thwarted inspiration by fragmenting her work. Even so, she accomplished a whole series of works that represent Thérèse as sacristan, as first communicant, in the midst of her Carmelite sisters, with the Child Jesus. She painted herself at her side. Let us mention especially the picture—which gave her a great deal of trouble because of certain difficulties with her eyesight—of Thérèse covering her crucifix with roses. This subject, painted in 1912, was inspired by the wish of the Postulator of the Cause that the custom be followed of discerning in the Servants of God some symbolic attribute. Then came the little apotheosis of the beatification, then of the canonization, and how many others!

Sister Geneviève was not unaware of the criticism that was repeatedly leveled against her by critics on the outside. Obviously, her tastes have to be judged by the standards of the times. Cloistered life made it difficult for her to update her standards of artistic judgment. She always lacked that advanced artistic training that her father, at one time, wanted to give her. Nevertheless, she made good use of the genuine gifts that were hers. Certain experts, standing before one or another of her canvases, have praised her technique; they have confirmed that the artist had talent.

In the introduction already mentioned, Father Francis of Holy Mary recognized that Céline's desire to make her model more attractive, which has often been reproached, was in reality only the desire, in itself quite legitimate, to capture and convey, beneath the veil of an extremely mobile countenance, something of what was eternal in that ideal soul. He regretted that such an effort, in which portrait painters of genius like a Velazquez, a Hans Holbein, a Quenton de la Tour, a Gainsborough triumphed, did not in this case have at its service either the sound technique or the aesthetic training that it demanded. Having made these reservations, he nonetheless pays homage to the work she did:

> Thérèse has nevertheless used these pictures to make her presence felt throughout the entire world, from the remote huts in the bush country to the tents of the nomads, and into igloos . . . to exercise there her gracious influence.
>
> Because of this, Céline's portraits merit our respect. They will always belong to the religious folklore of mankind and will continue to arouse interest in future ages, so true it is that the "spirit or the honest effort of an artist, who, no matter how, tries his best with the means he has at his disposal, not to become visible himself, but

to 'answer' the word by a word, the question by an action, and the Creator by something created",[2] and enters into the design of God and the work of salvation.

A renowned theologian was not afraid to write, some years ago: "If the well-known portrait of the Saint, which at first sight attracts attention and immediate interest, and which initiates the conquest of so many souls, contributes to making conversions, it is because it is infinitely peaceful and at the same time singularly profound."[3]

[2] Claudel, *Positions et propositions* (Paris: Gallimard, 1935).

[3] Father Petitot in his *Vie intégrale de Sainte Thérèse de Lisieux* (Paris: Éd. de la Revue des Jeunes, 1925), 6.

Upon entering Carmel, Sister Geneviève received, and occupied for many years, a cell facing out on the terrace, its window seen here on the far right; the cell of Saint Thérèse of the Child Jesus is marked with a cross.

5

Lights and Shadows on Carmel

I. Development of Devotion to Saint Thérèse

The worldwide spread of devotion to Saint Thérèse and the increasing number of pilgrimages to Lisieux made it necessary to consider building an edifice capable of accommodating large crowds of people. On a hill that had been drained, drilled, and reinforced with cement shafts about seventy-two feet deep, a basilica was raised whose foundation stone was laid on September 30, 1929. Sister Geneviève followed the work with passionate interest. She was an expert at deciphering the plans and comparing them with reality. It was she who drew up the designs that inspired the sculptors who erected the two Ways of the Cross, one in the apse of the sanctuary and the other in the crypt.

It was also necessary to think about the "spiritual basilica", as Canon Germain said when he built the Hermitage of Saint Thérèse. Sister Geneviève did her part, with Mother Agnes of Jesus, by seeing to it that the Thérèsian message was propagated. In the community council, she supported with all her might the initiatives of the Central Office in printing books, pamphlets, and doctrinal works. In this spirit, she accepted the burden of a vast correspondence that put her in touch with a great many people of renown from Rome, across the Channel, and across the Atlantic as well as from France. She found it more difficult to tolerate the visits to the parlor and the interviews imposed on her by certain ecclesiastical dignitaries who had been admitted into the cloister. To be "treated like some strange animal", as she said, made her rebel. She never did get used to it; she was less flexible in this regard than Mother Agnes of Jesus, who had the meekness that her name suggested. It was extremely displeasing to her to be thought of as a "great attraction" for those eminent personages occasionally ushered inside.

There were other grounds for annoyance. Extremely sensitive to anything that touched on Thérèse—pilgrimages, sanctuaries, biographies, statues, portraits—she endured piercing criticisms fired at the Carmel from certain quarters. Even an insulting suspicion with regard to the sisters of the Saint seemed to her to be the profanation of a memory and the violation of a doctrine. Only the spirit of the "little way" succeeded in restoring her serenity. She confided to Mother Agnes of Jesus:

> I don't know how to show my gratitude to God for putting us, like Jesus, through humiliation. I feel I will bless him for it throughout all eternity. Down here, I thank him for it with a joyful soul. I believe there are no graces greater than that. Ecstasies and miracles seem trite compared to that. Besides, I thrill with happiness to recall all that has happened in my life that made me fall, all that contributed to humbling me, even my faults, since they could not disfigure what is used for loving more.

From Rome came substantial compensations. Pius XI, the Pope of genius and "intrepid faith", had made Thérèse the star of his pontificate. Acknowledging that the Saint of Lisieux had miraculously cured him, he thought briefly about going there to thank her personally. For the solemn blessing of the basilica on July 11, 1937, he sent as legate his closest associate, the Cardinal Secretary of State himself.

The meeting with Cardinal Pacelli was for Céline an unforgettable event. In his discourse, he had said in particular: "Saint Thérèse of the Child Jesus has a mission, she has a doctrine. But her doctrine, like herself, is humble and simple; it consists of these two words: spiritual childhood, or these two words equivalent to it: little way." The joy of Sister Geneviève was at its peak on hearing these affirmations, which confirmed her deepest convictions.

July 12, when the papal legate visited the community, was another very special day. Only the pen of Céline could express this scene without losing anything of its charm.

A short time after Cardinal Pacelli's Mass in the infirmary, I got ready to take his photograph in the cloister. Alone with him, I asked him discreetly to pose under the archway I was pointing to, and when I had taken the picture, I drew near to thank him. His Eminence addressed a few kind words to me, congratulating me on being the sister of the little Saint. I told him my age, which surprised him. Then respectfully taking his hand and kissing it as if it were that of the future pope, I said to him: "Your Eminence, you are going to be pope after Pius XI, I'm sure of it. I am praying for that."

He answered very seriously: "Ask rather that I will have the grace of a happy death. That's more precious to me. May the good God be merciful and kind to me at that supreme moment."

I immediately resumed: "When one walks in the little way of spiritual childhood of our little Saint Thérèse, there is room only for confidence. She said that 'there would be no judgment for children and that one can remain a child in even the most formidable offices.' Besides, God does not want you to die so soon; there will be so much good for you to do when you are the Vicar of Jesus Christ."

Then, he appeared thoughtful, and said to me with extreme kindness: "No, there are a few obstacles to that; it is not likely."

At that moment, we were interrupted. But this conversation left me with an indelible memory.

On March 2, 1939, when the radio informed the world of the election of Pius XII, Sister Geneviève of the Holy Face recalled with emotion the dialogue in which she had played the prophet.

II. During the World War

Around that time, Europe, as if seized by a mass hallucination, rushed toward the Second World War. The decisive events were not long in coming: the invasion of Poland, mobilization, hostilities.

The alarming news that came from all parts of the world detached Céline more and more from earth. She longed for eternity. She found herself preceded there by her elders. For a long time, Sister Marie of the Sacred Heart, afflicted with rheumatoid arthritis, had known nothing but the infirmary and the wheelchair in which she was placed in order to move her. Sister Geneviève kept her company during recreation. She had the knack for keeping the interest of that generous but independent soul, for whom immobility constituted the worst penance. On one particular day, when she had invoked the example of M. and Mme. Martin's heroic courage and quoted, in support, these words from Maccabees: "Oh! do not sully our glory; do not allow it to be tarnished!", the "dear Godmother", filled with emotion, said to her devoted attendant: "Did you hear her! How eloquent she was! What a beautiful soul she has! Little Thérèse saw the truth of her, even through all her faults. And Father Pichon often said to me, 'Your Céline is a vessel of election!' " Sister Marie of the Sacred Heart died peacefully, in her eightieth year, on January 19, 1940. On the morning of her death, and in the week that followed, Sister Geneviève, inundated by mysterious perfumes, understood how "the death of saints is precious in the sight of God."

From that time on, she took Marie's place as the principal correspondent with Léonie. This did not last long, however, for Sister Françoise-Thérèse died on June 16, 1941, at the Visitation Convent at Caen. She was about to reach her seventy-eighth year. Céline, who envied the fortune of her departed sisters, reiterated in their regard the Norman proverb with which her father had once greeted the vocation of each of his daughters: "One more pulled from beneath the cart." She immediately added: "When will my turn come?"

The collapse of the Allied forces under German attack from air and ground, the occupation of the major part of the territory, the national humiliation, and the insolent triumph of Hitler's forces bruised the ardent heart of the Carmelite. In this deluge of fire and blood, would Lisieux be spared? On May 31, 1940, Sister Geneviève confided to Mother Agnes of Jesus her impressions and the reactions of her faith: "Humanly speaking, all seems lost, and we have every right to ask ourselves what is going to become of us and the relics of which we are the guardians. As far as we are concerned, it matters little because it would be a great good to cross over to the eternal shore toward which all our thoughts tend. But our treasures, I mean those precious relics of our little Thérèse? For a long time, I was preoccupied about that, and I suffered great anguish on their account. But now, I am no longer preoccupied. . . . The time has come when our little Thérèse is loved in spirit and in truth. So there is no real need for our senses to touch and see."

Céline grieved for France with equal distress. M. Martin's patriotism lived once again in her. There was, however, nothing chauvinistic about this. She showed no tolerance for the naïve arguments, filled with national pride, that pleaded on the basis of France's past as the "soldier of God throughout history" in order to endow it with a kind of credit account over heaven itself. Sister Geneviève meditated on the destiny of empires and their precariousness.

> I think [she wrote] that if God chastises us, it is because we are dear to him. . . . France is very guilty and, consequently, very ill. It is a mercy that God has decided to allow her to continue. . . . I beg him to extend his arms in order to save us, not because of our merits, but because of his goodness. I say that because I am shocked when I hear the virtues of France being praised excessively, as if, because of them, God were indebted to us. I would much prefer to see the just, with all their justice, follow the counsel of our Lord by admitting they are "unprofitable servants" and humbly taking his hand.

Collective pride, often unconscious or admitted with extreme levity, appeared to Céline as the most incurable form of pharisaism. "France", she said, "is humiliated, and this humiliation is a greater grace for her than the victory that would have intoxicated her."

In this period of recollection, when the poverty of war interrupted work, when pilgrimages and correspondence themselves slackened off, Sister Geneviève did not remain inactive. Searching through her archives and refreshing her memory, which continued to be surprisingly young, about precise details, factual anecdotes, and characteristic customs, she gathered together abundant documentation that facilitated the publication of the *Histoire d'une Famille* (The story of a family). The reverence she had for her father prompted her to use facts to contradict the flippant or malicious insinuations that surrounded his memory. When the work was drafted, she took a personal interest in the many illustrations destined to enhance the text. It was truly her book.

Other concerns were not long in claiming her attention. The Allied landing at Arromanches quickly placed Lisieux in the combat zone. From June 6 to August 22, 1944, some ten bombardments destroyed two thousand one hundred homes out of two thousand eight hundred, demolishing, along with two churches, most of the religious houses and killing more than a tenth of the entire population. In the evening of June 7, fire destroyed the chaplain's house and the Central Office, threatening the Carmel itself and its chapel. They had to seek a less precarious shelter in the crypt of the basilica. Leaning on the arm of one of the sisters, Sister Geneviève slowly made her way up the hill. She was peaceful and calm. "Since I can do nothing about it, I don't fret over it. If our whole monastery disappeared, its spirit would still remain." Just as she was uneasy even in little things when it was a question of her own initiative, so she showed herself detached when events rested in God's hand alone. That is what she said a few days later when one of the Lisieux townspeople announced that another bomb would inevitably hit the Carmel. "That is no longer up to us; let us abandon ourselves to the Lord for everything he will permit. He has always had pity on us. We can have complete confidence in him." In fact, at each approaching calamity, a gust of wind diverted the danger. It was as if an invisible hand had saved from destruction the sacred cluster of buildings that formed the Carmel, the House of Saint John, and the Hermitage.

The Carmelites took up living quarters in the crypt, at the upper end of it, in the chapel on the right, which is dominated by a reproduction of the Virgin of the Smile. A hundred persons or so, a number increased at times by people passing in and out, shared the remainder of the sanctuary. In spite of the discomfort of the place and the grim Matins chanted by shells and bombs, one can believe that the presence of the sisters of Saint Thérèse did not pass unnoticed. "These ruins should be entitled to remain in mystery", said

Sister Geneviève sulkily, extremely distressed by the excessive interest displayed in them. She spoke her mind about this to Mother Agnes of Jesus in this note dated July 7:

After fifty years of eremetical living, to find myself all of a sudden uprooted and thrown into the midst of the world, with veil raised, is a true martyrdom for a recluse like me. It seems to me as if we're in a station where everybody is crowding around and intermingling. We sleep fully clothed on benches; we take our meals in haste, standing up in the dark; we look with astonishment and grief at the feminine styles stripped of all dignity.

But that's not what makes life so hard; it is the visits! Everybody wants to see the sisters of Saint Thérèse and take turns coming to greet us. They keep pointing us out. Oh! that, that! little Mother, I can no longer stand. It seems to me, these days, that annoyances I feel about this are making me ill, and I call upon God to help me.

Once I was outraged; then during Office I thought gently on this passage from the holy Gospel: "Many Gentiles who had come up to Jerusalem to worship approached Philip and made this demand: 'My lord, we would like to see Jesus!' Philip went to tell Andrew; then Andrew and Philip told Jesus." That's what is taking place with us here at every moment; people are coming to tell us the same thing!

Then I was resolved to do as Jesus did and not to withdraw any more from those who wanted to see me, even if they were bothersome.

That did not prevent me from repeating after him: "Father, deliver me from this hour." But I am persuaded that, like him, "it is for this hour" that I have come here. Yes, I am certain that this trial was necessary for me at the end of my life.

Sister Geneviève, accustomed to handling accounts, records, and documents, found herself for the moment completely stripped and in danger of losing all her meticulously accumulated wealth of material. "But no matter," she says, "I feel deeply that it's all nothing, nothing. What does matter is

God's intervention; only his grace counts, and it does not need writing to penetrate and enlighten a soul. A little self-sacrifice practiced unobtrusively will open up the wellspring of it."

In this "apocalyptic dream", there were, even so, some intervals that afforded consolation. Mother Agnes and Sister Geneviève, forgetting their age, took advantage of breaks in the military situation to visit Les Buissonnets and the cemetery. They returned several times to their dear Carmel and even climbed to the top of the dome of the basilica under the watchful eye of Msgr. Germain.

More touching comfort was accorded them on June 13, when a messenger of Cardinal Suhard transmitted to the prioress a copy of a pontifical brief dated May 3, 1944, declaring Saint Thérèse of the Child Jesus secondary Patroness of France. Céline, always inquisitive, asked herself how the "little queen" could put so devastated a country on its feet again. "But in Joan of Arc's time," she exclaimed, "France was also very low. Saint Michael said to her: 'There is great compassion for the Kingdom of France!' And I was filled with hope and confidence."

Many steps were taken to get the Carmelites to accept evacuation with the relics of their Saint. Gently but firmly they refused; and, after the horrors of those final days, on Sunday, August 27, it was in procession across the ruins of the liberated city, carrying the reliquary, that they returned to their cloister.

III. In the Intimacy of Mother Agnes of Jesus

Conventional life resumed without delay in the midst of the necessary restorations. Sister Geneviève found her pen and her brushes again. At sixty-seven years of age, she painted portraits of Thérèse, as medallions on silk, for three chasubles that would be used for the jubilee of her profession.

Céline was in fact preparing to celebrate the half-century, heavy in history, that had passed since making her vows. On October 8, 1944, from the Carmel still bruised from its recent wounds, she wrote to a Roman prelate who was one of her confidants. Of so many memories full of glory, she wished to remember only her own wretchedness.

If I consider where I am, I notice that I have not gone forward but backward. . . . And there, I enjoy an astonishing peace even though it be in darkness. I take as my own this passage from a prayer of Saint Thomas Aquinas: ". . . At distant intervals, Lord, you draw me out of my lethargy, but alas! they are only passing visits. I do not know if you love me, or if I love you . . . I do not even know if I live by faith! I find only infidelity in myself, only random beginnings, only fruitless sacrifices . . . and yet, I long for you! . . ."

Oh! yes, I too, but I am not discouraged; and for many years I have taken comfort in this verse of Psalm 63, which we recite each Sunday at Lauds: "O God, my God! for you I long, for you my soul is thirsting. My body pines for you like a dry weary land without water. So I gaze on you in the sanctuary in order to contemplate your strength and your glory; for your mercy is better than life."

I feel this so deeply that, in my imperfection, although I regret it, I thrill with happiness at the thought that God's mercy is better than life. Perfection, the possession of virtues, spiritual consolations, I call "life"; and "death" is the state in which I now am, in that dry weary land without water, a state that does not prevent me, however, from approaching God with assurance, as if I were perfect, because I know it, I feel it: "His mercy is better than life." . . . Yes, I rely only on God's mercy and on his compassion; I want to arouse his compassion by my poverty, for I know that is how I will have gained all.

She often returns to this theme, seasoning it freely with lively and familiar phrases. Expressions like these repeatedly come from her pen: "I feel that I am queen of the imperfect. My kingdom is extremely vast, and I have myriads of subjects but, whatever they do, they cannot surpass their queen in this. . . . The fox will never change. Happily these words of my little Thérèse console me: 'It is enough to humble oneself, to bear one's imperfections with gentleness.' That is true sanctity for us."

On February 24, 1946, Sister Geneviève of the Holy Face celebrated her fifty years of religious profession. The chapel of the Carmel was hardly big enough to hold her many friends. The Apostolic Nuncio, Msgr. Roncalli, presided at the ceremony. He insisted on giving the crown and symbolic staff himself. His Excellency, Bishop Picaud, Bishop of Bayeux, preached the sermon, in which he skillfully analyzed Céline's kinship soul with Thérèse, a kinship that would continue providentially in heaven. He referred to the recent publication of *The Story of a Family* and, in his toast at the noonday meal, he publicly expressed the wish that M. and Mme. Martin would one day be glorified.

In the course of the monastery visit, the future pope was delicately attentive to Sister Geneviève. Playing pleasantly with the jubilee staff that she carried, he said to her: "Go before us, little Joan of Arc." And she led the ecclesiastical cortege through the convent premises, especially through those places that evoked memories of the Saint or where her relics were kept. Pope Pius XII very kindly sent his blessing to the jubilarian; it was inscribed at the bottom with an artistic watercolor that bore, along with his own shield, three pictures of Céline: one standing near Thérèse at the foot of Calvary, then painting the Holy Face, and finally kissing the hand of Cardinal Pacelli.

Sister Geneviève was even more touched by this passage of the handwritten letter that the Pope sent on the occasion of the fiftieth anniversary of Thérèse's death, on August 7, 1947, in which he spoke of spiritual childhood:

> Many think that it is a special way reserved to the innocent souls of young novices in order merely to guide them in their first steps, and that it is not suited to already mature individuals who need much prudence because of their great responsibilities. That is to forget that our Lord himself recommended this way to all children of God, even to those who have, like the apostles he formed, the greatest of responsibilities, that of the care of souls.

This pontifical testimony was all the more invaluable since at that time a well-intentioned but hastily written book, by a gifted novelist who certainly was not at all a historian, threatened to give the public a distorted picture of Thérèse as well as of her message. This work was the latest in a whole series of articles and biographies that exploited one-sidedly, by taking it out of context, the collective deposition made at the Thérèsian Process. It ended in defaming the Carmel, making Thérèse look hard, and warping her doctrine in a sense not exempt from heresy.

Mother Agnes of Jesus and Sister Geneviève protested with all the conviction of eyewitnesses. They dismissed no less vigorously every interpretation that tended to minimize spiritual childhood. In the perspective of their approaching death, Sister Geneviève drew up, on February 2, 1950, a text that was intended to be a definitive clarification and that bore, under her signature, the following written footnote: "Mother Agnes of Jesus has read, approved, and adopted this document on February 11, 1950." The better part of this text reads as follows:

Thérèse is the Saint of Love, but of a love that finds its most characteristic expression in spiritual childhood. She is the impassioned Saint of Jesus, but of a Jesus whose indescribable condescension she has opened to all little souls. She is the ingenious creator of the Act of Oblation to Merciful Love, which is within reach of the weakest souls who aspire only to "give pleasure" to God. Undoubtedly, we can see zeal for souls shine brightly in her; but, in order to win them over, she wanted to use those "little ways" that she dreamed of teaching to others, hidden sacrifices full of love and fidelity to everyday duties. . . . Let us repeat: her unique message, accepted, moreover, by the Sovereign Pontiffs as we have already observed, is the way of spiritual childhood.

Certainly it was her love that made her find this, at the height of her sanctity. But it was only after committing herself to it that she was inspired to offer herself as a victim to Love. All the saints are more or less heralds of Divine Love and of zeal for souls, while she alone is the herald of the "Little Way of Spiritual Childhood". That is her stroke of inspiration. That is her *Omen Novum*, her message, which I sum up here: joyful humility, passionate trust in Merciful Love, total abandonment to the divine will, a delicate art of giving pleasure to God in the least things of life, deep and experiential understanding of the Fatherhood of God, as I have testified during the Process in these words: "Her love for God the Father amounted to filial tenderness." Such is the secret of Thérèse's teaching. . . .

Faced with eternity, we who have lived in communion with Thérèse's thought insist on solemnly repeating: Thérèse's grace, her sanctity, and her mission is spiritual childhood.

On November 2, 1950, Sister Geneviève talked with Mother Agnes of Jesus about the autobiographical manuscripts that, altered and revised, had formed the *Story of a Soul*. Their complete publication, which had been considered at one time, had been postponed upon the intervention of the Holy See, in order not to impose upon the venerable prioress emotions that were beyond her strength. As Céline again began work on this edition, which would one day in fact be accomplished, just as the letters of the Saint had been at the end of 1948, her sister said to her: "After my death, I commission you to do it in my name."

Since the deaths of Marie and Léonie, the relationship between the last two surviving sisters became more intimate each day. Not only did they relive their past, but they shared ever more, in an indescribable peace, those secret thoughts that the approach of death awakens. "I love my little Céline more than anything else on earth", said Mother Agnes of Jesus, who, up to the end of her life, kept her gentleness and her gift of persuasion that, in her, blended so well with authority. "What would become of me if I did not have you", she confided to Céline on May 4, 1950; and, on the following August 6, along with her feast-day wishes: "You will have a happy death."

Sister Geneviève surrounded with tenderness and trust the one whom she so happily called "Little Mother", after the example of Thérèse. If she was pleased to talk with her, she also liked to put her thoughts into writing, according to the old Carmelite tradition. The letters she addressed to her on the occasion of her feast day or her birthday kept, up to the end, the simplicity and freshness that had made life so delightful at Les Buissonnets.

With fraternal solicitude, Céline watched over her elder sister during her last days. "She is as sweet and serene as possible, totally abandoned to God", we read in a note of June 2, 1951. "Yet I, who have known her in her prime, suffer at seeing her in this state of complete dependence; she can hardly stand upright, supported by two sisters."

When Mother Agnes of Jesus passed away the following July 28, in her ninetieth year, Céline felt her loss keenly; she was no less generous in offering up her loneliness:

> If I am stung with grief at the thought of my "Little Mother", I also have waves of joy in knowing that my whole family came out of the "great tribulation" victorious. I prefer to be the last one left. Then again, I am happy to give everything, everything to Jesus while I am still able to give. Complete stripping inside as well as out attracts me. Nothing becomes my all. I rely only on him.
>
> I notice very little here below [she continues writing]. My heart and my thoughts are truly in heaven without any sensible consolation. It is a strong and deep feeling. I am always talking to my "Little Mother". We two old women were fused together in these last years.

In order always to have Mother Agnes before her, she hung up on the wall of her cell a photograph, which she had framed, of Mother Agnes turning toward her Céline to smile at her.

One can imagine that this ultimate separation made the sense of eternity only increase for this last member of the Martin family. She had this delightful flash of inspiration. "We and our family have lived leaning out a window opening onto heaven." Close to the final day, she added:

> Besides the agony of death, simultaneous with it, a feeling of joy rises at the thought that I will have this witness to give to God. Yes, I think with pride on the passion that awaits me and that will precede my entrance into our homeland. It would be unfortunate indeed, I think, not to pass through death, for we can bear this witness only once, and it is precious in the eyes of God. Ah! what grace to have to prove to him our love by bearing witness! It is like the martyrs! Up until now I have been wanting in bearing this witness to Jesus as I wished; I have not practiced virtue as I would have liked; I have given witness only to my weakness and my im-

perfection. But, what joy! There still remains one witness to bear, and I do not want to miss *that* one!

"Welcome, Sister Death!" the Poor Man of Assisi had said.

6

The Advancing Years

I. The Octogenarian at Work

Having seen her whole family pass away, and herself more than eighty-two years of age, Sister Geneviève seemed called to spend the rest of her days in quiet repose under the care of a community who venerated in her the last echo of a marvelous past. Nothing of the kind happened. It was as if she had acquired new youth, and the last phase of her life overflowed with activity. Her faculties, which remained intact, submitted to incessant labor, capable of crushing the most vigorous and mature temperament. This beautiful longevity, which was nothing short of a miracle, prolonged Céline's mission in a providential way.

And yet, underneath her astonishing vitality, she hid health that had long been broken. From 1900 onward, rheumatism had deformed and stiffened her knees, later spreading to her shoulders, her neck, and her jaw. In 1942, there were attacks of sciatica and, a little later, gout, which pierced her for hours at a time in her hands and feet. Stomach trouble and liver complaints were frequent, along with pulmonary complications. To this were added insomnia and heart failure. The elderly sister suffered also from a loss of hearing and eyesight that was particularly painful for someone so eager to be informed and to communicate. During one period, Sister Geneviève knew what it was to have sleepless nights spent in an armchair saying her rosary or interrupted by getting up repeatedly to try to find a little relief! She willingly joked about her condition, using sayings from Les Buissonnets: "It's always the same. . . . A long illness wearies the doctor." She compared herself to a "pincushion full of needles". "Like Naaman, I would have to go and bathe seven times in the Jordan in order to regain my health." Borrowing the expression that the martyr Ignatius of Antioch had used to describe his fierce jailers, she speaks of the "ten leopards", various kinds of infirmities and trials that jealously attended her. She drew up a balance sheet of them: "What deficiencies in an old lady! What a procession of incapacities accompanies her! But how much profit must be in it since God allows them to exercise control over us, he who is so grieved to see us suffer."

In February 1953, a severe bout of influenza threatened her life. Aggressive treatment put her back on her feet. She was almost angry with the doctors who bustled around her bedside, happy besides to marvel at her philosophy and to receive her flashes of wit. "I am in an abyss of misery", she confided. "Am I going to pull myself out of it? Surely. Oh! how hard it is always to miss the train! . . . Nothing can go more slowly than the state I'm in now. I keep asking God not to let me to lack confidence. My soul is struggling in the lower depths. . . . I am always losing; when will I win?"

Since 1933, Sister Geneviève had occupied a cell on the ground floor, which spared her some fatigue. Upon the death of Sister Marie of the Sacred Heart, she was placed permanently in the infirmary, where her elder sister had endured long and terrible sufferings. In her last years, she was no longer able to participate in the Office or at community recreation. On February 6, 1951, she was able to obtain, because of her increasingly poor eyesight, permission to replace the breviary with recitation of the Our Father. She also found herself forced to cut down on her visits to the parlor. It must be noted that all the publicity that surrounded her annoyed her to the point of exasperation. During the period when permission to enter the cloister was obtained more easily, she literally fled visitors, disappearing at their arrival or appearing only at the last minute.

She spent all her energy struggling to assert the importance of Thérèse's message. She drew up a memorandum establishing how Thérèse had conceived the idea of her little way of spiritual childhood, with human influences playing only a secondary role in this regard and God alone serving as its inspiration. She devoted many articles to defining the exact meaning of the Act of Oblation to Merciful Love. Once again she gave the Thérèsian exegesis of the terms "Victim", "Holocaust", and "Martyrdom of Love" as a call to suffering, which had at first frightened Sister Marie of the Sacred Heart. She recalled the interpretations given by the Saint herself, which clearly distinguished the offering to Merciful Love from the offering to Justice, thus opening the way to the legion of little souls. Obviously, Céline was touching on a main point here about which she felt it necessary to dispel any ambiguity. The very spirit of the way of childhood was at stake. She who had seen, understood, and experienced Thérèse's examples and instructions could not refrain from speaking. She was conscious of defending the tradition in all its purity.

It was with this same disposition that in 1952 she published, under the title *Conseils et souvenirs*, the collection of papers in which she had gathered together the words and deeds of her sister when, as a young nun, she herself had lived with her and profited by her direction. The preface expresses the spirit of the undertaking:

"Only spiritual childhood . . . can give us true peace of heart" — *Sister Geneviève of the Holy Face*

I have reread and organized my memories, which were recorded in personal notebooks and in my preparations for the Depositions for the two Processes.

These texts, most often in dialogue form, give, as the *Imitation* says, the true tone of "the voice of nature" and "the voice of grace". And although on certain subjects "the voice of nature" is repeated to the point of becoming tedious, I have desired to suppress none of it so as not to lose any of the wise responses of the "voice of grace".

May these actual remembrances serve to help in a small way souls who struggle with their faults or imperfections!

I testify to the fact that these pages are truly consistent with what I have seen and heard.

In summary, while frankly disclosing all her weaknesses, Céline nobly agreed to serve as a foil to the ideal image of Thérèse's sanctity. Or better still, she meant to show in a concrete way how it was possible, despite serious handicaps, to progress along the "little way". She disclosed herself so bluntly that it was suggested to her that she depersonalize the account, veiling in anonymity certain passages that put her in too unflattering a light. She asked to think about it, and the next day she declared in a very definite tone of voice: "No, leave things as they are. The fact that the whole world will see that I have faults is no reason to have another one." To a friend who confided to her her astonishment and grief at seeing the contrast between the two sisters so plainly emphasized, she responded with her fine candor: "Our Thérèse had to reach a high level of perfection quickly; and she led us, me above all, her Céline, by the path she followed. . . . God allowed her apparent strictness not to discourage me but to incite me to perfection. It was in his designs that my virtues and graces would be 'slow' in coming. With Thérèse, the 'bomb' of graces exploded on the spot!"

Understood in this spirit, the work is essentially practical. It is in no way a treatise on spirituality or asceticism: lively anecdotes, recorded conversations, assorted confidences of valuable lessons; life tapped at the source and given as example. In all its two hundred pages, we find there the pedagogy of spiritual childhood. The mistress of novices is caught in real life portrayed in her little realm. She speaks, she acts, she counsels, she corrects, she gives herself completely, striving to carry along in her footsteps one whose hesitations and difficulties, admitted straight out, provoked the responses that clarify and stimulate. All the essential virtues are thus examined: humility, trust, love of God, fraternal charity, zeal for souls, fidelity to the Rule, poverty, self-denial, and fortitude in suffering. This last refers to the final illness and death of the Saint.

The volume of *Conseils et souvenirs* brought to a happy close the autobiographical manuscripts, the correspondence, and the *Novissima Verba* of Thérèse. It is like a series of snapshots in which we discover her without affectation or pretension, intuitive, lively, springing forth, with an incomparable self-mastery. Several successive editions have not exhausted the appeal of a work that is within easy reach of the least educated and yet gives satisfaction to the learned themselves, for it reveals just below the surface a sound and unerring doctrine.

Other works were already preoccupying our Carmelite. Recent writings, echoing unrestrained rumors, tended to put M. Martin in a false light, presenting him in his own household as a sort of secondary individual, half-ascetic, half-dreamer and totally devoid of common sense and vigor. These insinuations made Céline indignant; she was in a better position than anyone else to assess her father's moral worth; his courage, which, at times, bordered on temerity and made his family uneasy; and, finally, his unquestioned authority.

How could the truth be restored? On the other hand, a whole movement, coming particularly from across the sea, urged the glorification of Thérèse's parents. The Carmel, knowing the concerns and efforts entailed in pursuing a Cause, proved rather hesitant. Yet it was important not to let the most authoritative witness disappear without taking down her deposition under oath before ecclesiastical authority. This is what led Sister Geneviève to dig into the dusty records for everything that concerned M. and Mme Martin. She could be seen, at eighty-four years of age, toiling over a whole pile of papers with a magnifying glass, working up two booklets that appeared in 1953 and in 1954, which were entitled: "The Father" and "The Mother of Saint Thérèse of the Child Jesus". After having drawn up the moral portrait of these noble Christians, Céline stressed their sickness and death. She also included in the appendix, along with a sketch, valuable topographical details of the house and garden on the rue Saint-Blaise in Alençon. Those who witnessed this lengthy effort at clarification and composition were altogether edified by the youthful fervor and the strict historical integrity of this author.

To be sure, these publications added nothing new to the biography of Thérèse's parents. Their value lies above all in that ardor, spontaneity, and simplicity that Sister Geneviève put into everything she did. Were these testimonials enough to dismiss the myth? One may doubt it, since false rumors are difficult to dispel; there is always something apocryphal lurking around the dwellings where sanctity comes to life. Sister Geneviève had scarcely any illusions in this regard. "The false statements", she writes in her letter of introduction, "pass from mouth to mouth and end by covering up the truth completely, like successive layers of sediment hiding the shell and the splendor of its pearly luster."

On July 11, 1954, the solemn consecration of the Thérèsian sanctuary took place, which, by decree of the Holy See, was raised on this occasion to the dignity of a minor basilica. Sister Geneviève had herself been employed, through a mountain of correspondence, in obtaining, from the different countries that had offered an altar, relics of saints, which she herself put into the different little containers to be sealed in the stone. She listened with gratitude to the radio message in which Pius XII praised the Carmelite and recommended to all her followers the humility, confidence, and love that characterize her little way.

This event imparted new life to Thérèsian studies. With pontifical approbation, the complete facsimile edition of the autobiographical manuscripts was busily prepared. It came out in 1956 and excited tremendous interest in the Catholic world. Sister Geneviève, who, more than anyone else, encouraged this publication and kept a very close watch on the laborious critical editing, rejoiced at its success.

She was led to revise another work that had been out of print for some time and that needed to be completed and adapted in view of recent publications. This involved fusing together an incalculable number of texts coming from very nearly everywhere. To obtain them, to look into their authenticity, to restore them to the original, and to regroup them required an almost superhuman effort considering the conditions under which Sister Geneviève toiled: half-blind, hands numb, and unable to get around easily. She herself said that it was too much for her.

She had to face another kind of trial. On February 24, 1956, she marked the sixtieth anniversary of her profession. For some time, there had been a good deal of whispered talk about this diamond wedding anniversary. She wanted to avoid this "bugbear jubilee", as she called it. At her wish, the gifts received on this occasion were contributed toward the renovation and embellishment of the liturgical treasures of the basilica. On the dreaded day, a simplified ceremony took place in the chapel of the Carmel, presided over by His Excellency, Bishop Jacquemin, Bishop of Bayeux. The sermon was delivered by the Very Reverend Father Marie-Eugène of the Child Jesus, former Apostolic Visitator of the French Carmelites. An autographed papal blessing, two letters—one from Cardinal Ottaviani and the other from the Very Reverend Father General of the Discalced Carmelites—highlighted the event.

Three days later, the jubilarian suffered an attack of influenza that threatened her life. For six months, almost continuous suffering tormented her nights. She bore it peacefully, doing everything possible not to disturb her infirmarian. She was encouraged by thinking of the martyrs, especially Saint Sebastian, who, delivered miraculously from death, confronted his persecutor a second time and received the martyr's crown twice. "It is incredible how God helps me", she confided. "I would never have wanted to ask him for suffering, but now I thank him."

Thus debilitated, it seemed that a new crisis would promptly overcome her. "I have gone down into the valley of the shadow of death", she wrote. "Truthfully, I fear nothing about it, and I am quite abandoned to it without being conscious of it." Contrary to all expectations, she rallied. Toward the end of April when, for the second time, the general assembly of the Federation of the French Carmels met at Lisieux, she again had to receive some two hundred and sixty superiors and delegates who were permitted to visit the interior of the monastery. She consented to this stream of visitors with good grace, careful, despite her fatigue, to give each one a personal mark of interest.

II. M. and Mme Martin's Cause

Other tasks awaited her. On the same day as her jubilee, Bishop Jacquemin had made known to Sister Geneviève his intention of authorizing the opening of the informative process of the Cause of Louis Martin. On March 22, 1957, he signed the order for the examination of the writings of the Servant of God. The Bishop of Sées, the Most Reverend Pasquet, did the same for Zélie Guérin. If one wanted to avoid the labyrinth of a historical process, it would be of the utmost importance to question the last living witnesses.

Provided with the Articles[1] that directed the investigation, Céline prepared herself for the interrogations with the same conscientiousness she bestowed upon everything. She freely said that she was interested only in the Causes of persons who had a mission: for example, Joan of Arc, Liberator of France; Thérèse, messenger of spiritual childhood; Maria Goretti and Dominic Savio, witnesses and apostles of purity. If she wished to see her parents glorified—both of them at the same time, in distinct but morally paired processes—it was so that the model of an ideal household might be proposed for the family, which was increasingly threatened with disintegration.

Thus she gave evidence before the Tribunal of Bayeux, which was located, for the occasion, in the parlor of the Carmel, and which, besides acting on its own behalf, acted also by rogatory commission on behalf of the Tribunal of Sées. Sister Geneviève was interrogated at the beginning of April and in June for M. Martin; then in November and

[1] This name refers to the overall plan established, in view of the Informative Process, by the Postulation for the Cause; it sets forth the life of the Servant of God, his heroic virtues, and his reputation for sanctity. It is a basic document that clarifies the entire debate.

December 1957 for Mme Martin, in a number of sessions, several of which lasted up to four hours. She speaks of a day when she was "under cross-examination for seven hours". The judges admired her presence of mind and relished more than once the incisive remarks and the reminiscences of old Norman folklore with which she peppered her declarations. As far as she was concerned, she was surprised that she was able to withstand the fatigue so cheerfully.

In February, August, and September 1958, she again intervened in the Process of non-cult[2] and of the writings. On September 6, she made her last deposition. On this same day, having carefully reread all the proofs, she approved Mme Martin's correspondence for printing. Her plan for the erection of a statue of Thérèse in the middle of a garden in line with the road that leads to Les Buissonnets was finally executed. On September 12, she determined to go up to the attic, where certain trunks of family records were kept. She had wanted to do this exploring for several years.

On October 13, 1958, in the presence of the Bishop of Bayeux, of the Most Reverend Pioger, Auxiliary Bishop of Sées, and the Most Reverend Fallaize, former Vicar Apostolic of MacKenzie, the remains of M. and Mme Martin were exhumed and transferred to the plateau of the Way of the Cross near the apse of the basilica. Sister Geneviève was moved to learn that the only object found intact on each of the bodies, outside of a metal crucifix, was the Scapular of Our Lady of Mount Carmel. More poignant still was the observation, made by the three doctors, of deep vertebral lesions in Mme Martin on a level with the left shoulder blade, where the can-

[2] The Process *de non-cultu* is a part of the process of canonization. Along with the examination of the person's writings, it is part of the second step in the preliminary process to determine sanctity. An examination is made to determine that there was a previous absence of public honor given to the person.

cer had worked its terrible ravages. Evidence of heroism was registered in the skeleton.

It was then necessary to gather up, to sort, to wash with alcohol and to classify under a wax seal the dust and debris contained in the coffin, without removing anything except the bones, which were enclosed in new tombs. Sister Geneviève, along with her infirmarian, busied herself with this exhausting, meticulous labor into which she put all her filial piety. On December 12, she was still cutting cardboard with extraordinary difficulty and preparing, for these souvenirs, boxes of different sizes and the appropriate labels. Literally, she was at the end of her strength, but with the very peaceful sense that her task was at last finished.

For some time, without anyone around her noticing it, she had felt that she was aging terribly. She saw in this a source of blessings. She showed more serenity than in the past in putting up with changes. Speaking of certain ornaments that she had long taken care of and that the modern taste for simplification had set aside, she said: "I thank God for allowing me to see this in my lifetime and for enabling me to be lovingly detached from it."

"The form of this world is passing away", she repeated in the face of certain traditions that had become outdated and at the sight of old customs pushed to the background. Her whole impulse carried her toward heaven. The verse from the Apocalypse: "Behold, I am coming soon. Yes, I am coming soon", thrilled her. The approaching dénouement filled her with great hope. "It's not that I want to be delivered from suffering and work", she explained; "It's finally to be near my Jesus, whom I have loved for so long a time; near the Blessed Virgin, my dear Mother, and Saint Joseph; in order to know at last all the details of their life here on earth."

Her confidence remained unshaken. On December 8,

1958, she was still writing: "My nights are often painful, my days filled with work. 'One thing follows another.' All of that, together with the thousand little miseries of old age, is a burden I do not often take up with a smile, but rather with a sigh. I would not want God to hear it. And yet, I look upon all my imperfections as treasures, and I summon them to appear at my judgment, for all my faults are my strength. Since I regret them and am sincerely humiliated by them, I think that they will draw God's pity down upon me; and when he has pity, he also has mercy."

She savored the beautiful book of Msgr. Baunard, *Le Vieillard* (The old man). She discovered this stanza in it, which she enthusiastically applied to herself:

I am nearing a hundred, my day draws to a close;
It is more than evening, it is almost night.
But, in front of me, rises in the east
The dawn of a more beautiful day. Welcome, welcome!
It is the white light of your face, O Christ,
Which in my sad heart awakens a great hope;
Come down, heavenly ray, appear, my Brother,
Jesus, it is time for us to see each other.

7

The Intrepid Heart of a Child

I. A Great Personality

Sister Geneviève of the Holy Face was a character. Alert and alive, with observant eyes under very pronounced arched eyebrows; a strong chin and well-formed lips with a slightly imperious pucker; a watchful, or one might say guarded, face: this is how she appeared to the visitors who were privileged to see her in the parlor. Mother Agnes of Jesus sketched her portrait in this verse, which in French formed an acrostic of her name:

> Céline, brave knight without reproach and without fear,
> Espoused to Jesus and Thérèse's sister dear.
> Heaven [*Le ciel*] is in her name, divine art in her soul;
> There are no [*Il n'est pas*] mysteries her fervor does not
> penetrate
> Nor beauty that she would not wish to love;
> In the end [*En fin*], humility alone could charm her.

The last line refers to the work that grace performed in her soul in the name of spiritual childhood; the first line describes a straightforward and strong nature, ready for combat. This contrast will shine forth throughout the chapter, which attempts to touch on the moral traits of our Carmelite, before she leaves the scene.

It would be an understatement to say that she was headstrong and opinionated. She was a person capable of making quick decisions and of being tenacious and spirited in carrying them out. She knew nothing of vague approximations; she liked neither delays nor compromises, yet knew how to use her Norman finesse when needed to gain her own ends. In order to cope with her many tasks, she had to expend an incredible amount of energy. When she was almost eighty, she could be seen going upstairs to the archives, leaning on her cane, searching through a trunk, opening and examining a pile of records in order to find again one date, one line, one text, so conscientious was she in her work. She was most certainly not one of those "languid persons who constitute", she said, "a deadweight, one who bridles the general spirit!" Rather, she reproached herself for interfering with too much impetuosity.

I noticed with admiration [she writes] that, in her last years, Sister Marie of the Sacred Heart permitted all kinds of opinions to be expressed in front of her at recreation without ever saying anything herself. She remained there calm and serene in her little wheelchair while I could not keep from jumping in and saying straight out what I thought. That still happens to me despite my seventy-two years. "Daughter of thunder" I will be, alas! always sensitive to atmospheric emanations; and God will be obliged to take me as I am, vibrant and warlike.

Some months before her death, she flew into a rage against an unknown religious, guilty of having drawn, for the cover of a spiritual book, grimacing pictures that ruined the face of Christ and his saints: "I want to write to that sister and tell her that she has committed a veritable sacrilege."

This willfulness sustained her even in the intellectual sphere. Although deprived of higher education and special instruction, she liked to educate herself, to understand, and to get to the bottom of everything. She confessed it without equivocation: "I have always weighed and dissected the propositions set before me; I wanted proof of what had been put forward, and I was ill at ease as long as the question was not fully resolved."

Her curiosity was insatiable. She reacted to everything. In her later years, she undertook to read the *History of the Church* by Daniel-Rops; she gleaned information from the journal *Ecclesia*, from studies on missiology, and from *L'Ami du Clergé*; the biography of Dom Guéranger fascinated her; above all, she studied the Bible, delighted to compare three or four different translations; after the Gospels, the Epistles of Saint Paul constituted her bedside reading. At eight-nine years of age, she still annotated in writing the most beautiful verses from Saint John. Yet, at the same time, she was interested in the recent geological discoveries of the ice age and in the paleontological hypotheses about the age of humanity.

Whatever struck her was immediately written down on paper and classified. She owed that to her uncle Guérin. Besides, she was the first to joke about it, as seen in this rhyme addressed to Mother Agnes of Jesus:

> I am an old archivist,
> Of my treasures, long is the list.
> I know everything that exists.
> In throwing away nothing I persist,
> And, when necessary, I unexpectedly insist,
> I use everything like an artist.

Let us bless this gift that she calls "innate". It earned for us the preservation of invaluable documentation about Thérèse and her family.

Sister Geneviève was certainly not an idealist. Essentially

practical, she was remarkably ingenious in arranging and making use of things. As a child, upon returning from a walk, she cut the material of her doll dresses to make them like those she had carefully examined in the shop windows. And she was the one who, from a distance and on the basis of only a sketchy plan, at the beginning of the century when there were threats of expulsion, conceived the idea of restoring and fitting out the property acquired in Belgium by Dr. La Néele, for the benefit of the Carmel.

Céline was not vain despite her unquestionable talents. Quoting the scriptural example of Bezalel, whom "God filled with a divine spirit of skill and understanding and knowledge in every craft", she said: "The Lord is always the same; he gives us what we need; so I could be told that I had accomplished great things without taking pride in them." She knew how, when needed, to repress the first movements of self-love. Some of the workmen were amazed at the sketches she had drawn for them of a basin for developing and washing photographs. "That sister is a real architect", they exclaimed. Finding herself pleased with this praise, she mortified herself by renouncing for Jesus the pencil with the steel tip to which she was very much attached.

What Sister Geneviève had to watch, above all, was her extreme sensitiveness. She was quickly moved to enthusiasm; she had a need to confide in someone and to be understood. Loyal in friendship, the least attention aroused her gratitude; lack of consideration pained her deeply. Having little self-control, she did a poor job of hiding her irritation when she was interrupted in the midst of her work or when her plans were upset. Impulsive as she was, she was quick to answer back sharply without noticing whom she hurt. Realizing it afterward, she immediately—for she was fairness itself—made a humble confession of it. Her practiced eye detected promptly the virtues and faults of her neighbor; her retentive memory registered it. Such was nature's place in the balance sheet. She herself noted this with inexorable clarity, however, exaggerating the pejorative note.

On April 19, 1940, she wrote to Mother Agnes of Jesus, who loved to elicit and receive her confidences:

> I am drawing up for myself a little balance sheet called a precision balance (*trébuchet*), which is used in medicine to weigh milligrams, because it is perfectly true that I am sensitive to the least milligram and that even one milligram makes me stumble (*trébucher*). But I know very well that it will always be like that. I still feel that I will always be like quicksilver, doing things before I think them through. It is very unfortunate to have so little equilibrium and level-headedness because a host of imperfections are the consequence. But I think that God likes to cope with difficulties and that he is not embarrassed to make a passage for himself in the midst of a muddy abyss.

"I always wanted", she notes in her *Conseils et souvenirs*, "the details of my life to fit together like a puzzle. Anyone who disturbed them was in for trouble! If some unexpected circumstance happened to ruin the scheme and mix up the pieces, I showed my displeasure."

This was a very fair observation, but it lacks the other side of the picture, which must also be considered. Along with this indisputable liability, one must point out the credit of the at times heroic struggles that Sister Geneviève waged against herself, which those nearest to her readily observed. Each time she received Holy Communion, she begged, for that day, patience and kind judgment. Writing to a religious much younger than she was, and who was celebrating her silver jubilee of religious profession, she declared to her: "It is unnecessary for you to tell me to pray for you, but it is very necessary that I ask you to do so for me. Today, you have all claims over the Heart of your Spouse; ask him, then, to give me, not your meekness, for I would not want to deprive you of it, but a meekness similar to yours, a treasure I need very much."

On June 4, 1958, seven months before her death, she sent this note to one of her sisters whom she feared she had disedified: "Oh! how you touched me last night by your kindness, your meekness, your affection; me, who showed myself so headstrong; I ask your humble pardon!" And she signed it with the name her sisters loved to call her at Les Buissonnets: "Little repentant Céline".

If, at times, her retorts were feared, they most often brought a smile, for she had the art, in that melodic way that revealed Lower Normandy, of mixing them with spicy remarks and anecdotes that cheered her visitors in the parlor. Did she not appear to be full of amusing expressions meant to entertain those who came to visit her? To the compliments paid her by a physician, she replied with a solemnity laced with humor: "But . . . didn't you know that I was a great soul?" If some delicate matter was being discussed and nothing was being resolved, she would cry out: "Let's put it aside till tomorrow; it's at night that ideas come to me." Or else: "Let's talk nonsense. It's from the clash of ideas that light flashes out." If she happened to use an unusual term, she would exclaim comically: "What a word to come out of my mouth!", taking on the expression of a religious in times past. Once, in the course of a conversation on exterior faults, she threw out: "The Blessed Virgin herself would perhaps have gotten on our nerves by the way she put on her veil or her apron."

When someone spoke to her about a Servant of God whose biography was woven with sensational deeds, she would say, in the manner of Father Pichon: "That's not my kind of saint!" She even spoke ironically about her own deficiencies. "I need many prayers to become patient, but I will suffer the want of that virtue my whole life, and I will die without ever having enjoyed it; I feel it's hopeless. So, dying as I have lived, without patience, I will not be able to wait at heaven's gate, and I will go straight on through it." She compared herself to jackasses, whose stubbornness is proverbial, "which are not fastidious and walk no place in particular, over stones, in the mud, at the edge of precipices", not letting themselves be stopped by any difficulty.

II. The Child of the God of Love

The thing that is most attractive in her—Thérèse, as we have said, was very sensitive to it—was her direct, practical, sincere, and straightforward manner, in a word, her simplicity. She manifested it everywhere and in all circumstances, toward the little as well as the great. After being ecstatic over a nest of baby chicks or with the little white rabbits presented to her by the novices, she could easily carry on a conversation with a Prince of the Church. Dare we say that she acted the same way with Jesus? In her intimacy with him, she used the most familiar form of address. She longed for him with all her strength. "Oh! if only people could see nothing of myself in me but only Jesus!" She had the same familiarity with Mary, her "heavenly *Maman*".

At the end of her life, she was enraptured by a passage from Father Faber. She recognized herself in it trait for trait.

Simplicity comes very near to God, because boldness is one of his most natural graces. It comes near because it does not know what progress it is making. It thinks not at all of itself in order to consider its own unworthiness, and that is why it is precipitous, while a soul more conscious of its actions would advance only very slowly; the soul here is at full liberty, whereas another type of sanctity would wait for permission. These simple souls come to God with a sort of effrontery of love that fears nothing; and when they are near God, they simply rejoice and do nothing more. At times, I could almost say that there is something unceremonious about the manner in which these souls receive great graces and divine inspirations as being the most natural things, and the Holy Spirit seems to delight in their simplicity and their sincerity. These are perpetual children.

Here we have the magical word that throws light on Sister Geneviève's whole interior life. "It is the nature of children", she noted, "to live in humility and dependence, to have a simple spirit and a tender gratitude for the least favors, to accept without arguing what the father of the family prescribes just as it is also their virtue to fear nothing when they are under their father's protection." This was the ideal that Thérèse had communicated to her while she was living and still more after her death. She could have said to her: "It is good for you that I go away", for her sisterly influence turned out to be more determinative when her posthumous mission began. Céline, who was aware of this, also grasped admirably well the ingenious intuition that constitutes the key to spiritual childhood: Since God is merciful Love, misery attracts him and provokes a sea of graces; it is enough for us to recognize it, to accept it, to love it, and not to cease to offer to the Lord our ineffective efforts, which he will crown in his own good time.

Basically, it is an absolute faith in infinite Love. "I have God for myself", wrote Céline; "He is a Father to me, and I love him unto folly, passionately. . . . My only desire is to know him more and more, to attain to the ultimate limits of this knowledge on earth, and later in heaven . . . , and to do that, I feel it is necessary to attain the ultimate limits of humility;

which is why I keep begging for it so insistently. That sums up the whole of my poor little soul."

Although totally surrounded by the poetry of Christmas, the eighteenth-century hymn in which is sung: "Happy mystery! in which Jesus suffers for us to appease the wrath of a severe God", did not find favor with Sister Geneviève. Still less the sermons that, in the oratorical fashion of the day, put the rigorous Justice of the Father in opposition to the Mercy of the Son. She wrote to Mother Agnes of Jesus in February 1936:

> Yesterday evening I came from prayer with a heavy heart. I had meditated on the Passion in a new Life of Christ. It was a very grave mistake. My love for God was crushed with each line. In order for this not to be so, I would have to love him less and not have such a sense of his goodness; and that is real martyrdom. What I get out of this reading is the idea that God is severe, that he thirsts for the blood of his Son, who was made a victim for men. It speaks only of a bloody sacrifice, of expiation. Not one word of mercy or pardon. The debt for sin must be paid, "drunk to the last drop" to this inflexible Master, to this inexorable Judge. Truly, with the thoughts I have about God, I wonder if I am not a heretic. . . . But then, let him change my heart himself! As for me, I do not see "the great Victim of Calvary" as everyone else does. These interpretations hurt me. To rest from all of that . . . I go back to the Gospel, to Scripture, to my little Thérèse.

Christ, beforehand, had cleared Sister Geneviève of all suspicion of heresy: "Whoever sees me, sees my Father", he had said to Philip. So it is guided by Jesus that Céline goes to discover the Father. This name of Jesus was so dear to her that she pronounced it with loving tenderness. Above all, she marveled at the divine condescension: "When I was a child," she wrote in her autobiography, "I used to play with the daughter of the Prefect. But when she wanted my company, she sent her governess to look for me, or from her balcony she would motion for me to come over. She never came to our house. She made Thérèse and me 'go up' to her without ever 'coming down' to us. And God, himself, comes down. . . ." Giving her own commentary on the song of the angels at Bethlehem, that *Gloria* which ascended to heaven at the time when the Word of life "was humbled to the very depths", Sister Geneviève concludes: "God thus deems himself glorified when he is reduced to the point of becoming this little newborn infant in rags." She was there repeating the daring expression of Bossuet about the All-Powerful "who is enriched by humility".

In the face of such an example, how can one claim to exalt oneself? The wisdom of the publican is imperative. Céline wanted nothing else. "On what would I base my confidence? Ah! I know well what it is; it will be on my miseries, on my defects, on my faults themselves. It will be in procession with them that I present myself before God, full of assurance, because then his pity will be my portion. He will save me, not because of my good works, but because of his goodness."[1]

Céline did not acquire this attitude of mind overnight. In a poem dated in the month of August 1919, and entitled ". . . And Your God Will Be Your Glory", she happily re-

[1] It is useful to note that Sister Geneviève reasoned neither as a quietist, for whom passive abandonment is everything, nor as a Protestant for whom faith alone suffices, independently of works. She knew that one's faith must be active; she multiplied her efforts to correct herself, to sacrifice herself, and to please Jesus. But she knew also that these works had value only through the merits of Christ. That is why, imitating Thérèse, she based her hope of heaven only on infinite Love.

Likewise, when she declared that she relied on her misery, on her very faults, one must understand that, having courageously fought and suffered to conquer her faults, she was aware that God alone could free her from them, and that in his great Mercy, he would be moved to pity her in the measure that he saw her humble and poor; like a mother with respect to her sick child.

counted her spiritual journey. When her youth was awakened to the Beauty from on high, it was like the euphoria of personal victories.

> I wished, at that stage, like an athlete full of vigor,
> To win the prize quickly.
>
> I dreamed of running to take the virtues by storm.

The novitiate, under Thérèse's guidance, dispelled this presumptuousness and opened to her other perspectives:

> Yes, often, very often, falling on the way,
> I left a little of my wool in the bushes,
> And from humility, in the evening of the day
> I learned some lessons.
> Lessons without bitterness and full of hope,
> For if I am little, oh! how great Jesus is!
> I am weak; he is strong, and his superabundance
> Makes up for my nothingness.

More than splendid dreams! More than personal plans! Sister Geneviève left herself to Jesus, whom she would serve with all her might, without counting her own merits.

> I want you to be everything, everything in me,
> for I love you. . . .
> You are my ideal.

III. The Virtues of Childhood

In this light one can see the principal role that she assigned to humility. "Humility was always my favorite virtue, my friend and my counselor, and I was relentless in asking God to grant it to me." Not the crushing type of humility that borders on depression, but confident humility that relies on more than self. "I desire only one thing, and that is that God may have pity on me; and one can be pitied only when one is in a pitiable state."

Perhaps one will object that such remarks are facile and of little importance in a religious associated with the Thérèsian glory, surrounded, appreciated, and sought after like the living relic of a great past. This would be a complete misunderstanding. Not only did Sister Geneviève practice voluntary self-effacement, fleeing the parlor, shying away from displays of esteem, and suffering at being introduced to important personages, but she had known and accepted humiliation. She did not react during the long period of time when she was not permitted to be a member of the chapter. Nor when mistresses of novices were appointed who were younger than she, Mothers Marie-Ange of the Child Jesus, Isabelle of the Sacred Heart, and Thérèse of the Eucharist, who had not been trained in the school of the Saint as she had been. "If our Mother does not think of me," she was content to say, "it is because I have faults that I don't realize. I must submit without understanding."

Later on, it was from outside the cloister that trials came. She was said to have gone downhill, suffering from mental illness, transferred outside the monastery. It was at this point that the Reverend Father Rodrigue of Saint Francis de Paul, Postulator of Thérèse's Cause, gave instructions for her to be "brought forward". She then entered the council and, on this basis, accompanied the ecclesiastical dignitaries allowed to enter the cloister. One of them, as if astonished by her alert mind, let this remark slip out: "I must be the one who is crazy", the meaning of which was not lost on Céline. She, who always leapt forward when the memory of her family was attacked, remained serene when it was a question of herself.

The same disinterestedness was displayed on the subject of her works. We have already noted how much effort the book *The Spirit of Saint Thérèse* cost her. She nonetheless wrote to Léonie, after sending the manuscript to M. Dubosq: "I do not know if that's what they want, but if they burn it, I won't feel cheated. Since I acted only for Jesus I will always be well paid for my trouble." Toward the end of her life, she spent a long time drawing up a memoir on the way of childhood for a high-ranking Roman official. As luck would have it, the document, faithfully sent back, was lost at the Carmel and was never spoken of again. This silence surprised and pained her, but she did not breathe a word about it.

In a paper prepared in advance of her death, she wrote: "If our Mother does not want to do a circular for me, she may say that I requested it. It would make it easier for her. If, on the other hand, she intends to do one, may it be only in order to speak of my beloved Thérèse. May she know it pleases me to have my many faults made known in order to throw light on the incomparable virtues of my little sister. Just as, in a picture, shadows heighten its brightness, I consider myself blessed to serve in that same capacity for the glory of God and my Thérèse."

That "dreadfully everyday" cross was at times hard to bear. "I do not have the strength", sighed Sister Geneviève on August 6, 1939, at the dawn of the Feast of the Transfiguration.

But Thérèse spoke to her heart: "I have a peaceful feeling that my hope will be fulfilled, that I have nothing to fear here below because I will always have the strength not to have the strength, and that to know this was the feast-day gift from heaven to the little exiled Céline."

The principal object of her humiliation was the incessant struggle that she had to wage up to the end in order to conquer her too-lively sensitiveness, which at times burst forth outwardly. Since she was necessarily so much in the public eye, her moods could not pass unnoticed. They risked being discovered. She experienced neither distress nor bitterness about it. She was never seen to be discouraged or to endeavor to hide her "outbursts". She lived always faithful to the motto: "The one who loses wins", and loyally observed the rules of the game. She accepted seeing her soul reduced to a "pile" of rubble—it is the title of one of her most delightful poems—her dreams and illusions lying about on the ground, her virtues withering away on this sterile earth. But she counted on Love to purify everything and to make an authentic sanctity spring up from these ruins; the sanctity of Christ, who is "the only Saint".

Many passages could be quoted on this point. Let us choose these lines written in her later life in which she pleasantly speculated on her eighty-eight years. "My long life is drawing to a close in a pile of zeros. It is true that I have labored much, worked, suffered; but what are these works in themselves in a creature so imperfect as I am? Rubble. It is fortunate, indeed, if my zeros are not too often blotched with ink spots! But that quite corresponds to my desire to have only a page of zeros to offer to God. For I prefer that there be nothing to reward or to praise in me. I want to be clothed solely with the works of Jesus and for my heavenly Father to judge me and love me according to them."

Sister Geneviève of the Holy Face, 1957

The nearer she came to the end, the more simplified Sister Geneviève's interior attitude became, an attitude in which an analysis would discern both a side of humility and one of confidence but which was, in fact, a single movement, a filial impulse toward the paternal Heart. Shortly before her death, she confided to a friend: "I live the life of pure faith. . . . In the world, strangers think I am inundated with delights at the sight of the glory of our little Saint. What an illusion! I do not think I have ever been in such a spiritual desert." In spite of it all, she worked, she prayed, she struggled, she suffered, she offered up her nothingness, for her temperament was diametrically opposed to any kind of glum passivity.

I am nourished by this testament that has been bequeathed to me by my Thérèse: "It is Love alone that counts." And Love is total abandonment, the blind trust of a little child in its dear heavenly Father, which cannot work without a profound humility and which becomes, without anyone suspecting it, a natural virtue as it is in all little ones.

Our Thérèse leads us by her way; it is better even than if our last days were spent in ecstasy. I have always thought, and even desired, to have "my passion" before Jesus receives me into his arms.

What should I tell you about my soul? [she once asked a religious]. Nothing, nothing from heaven's side, not the least consolation. . . . It is true that I have peace of heart. That's the important thing. "The greatest grace that God can give us", says Saint Paul, "is not only to believe in him but also to suffer for him." That thought often comes to my mind and strengthens me in the midst of my darkness. I believe that this state of darkness is the prelude to the light into which we will soon enter.

Sister Geneviève had not forgotten the lesson of the lift. She anticipated the final gesture that would detach her from her miseries. On August 6, 1958, her last feast day on earth, she saw in a dream a languid stream, carrying along with it plant debris, that, on approaching the estuary, was purified, swelled, and came to life in an imposing mass of water, free from all impurities. "I think", she wrote, "that this is the image of my poor life, so encumbered by all sorts of imperfections that my Jesus will make disappear when he sets it right, at the moment when I throw myself into his arms." This hope would not be frustrated; the following section will fully bear this out.

IV. The Problem of Suffering

Céline had inherited from her sister her unabashed certainty of "the great love" of God. Two scriptural verses serve as refrains. She placed them as epigraphs at the top of one of her notebooks. "Blessed be God, the Father of mercies, the God of all consolation, who consoles us in all our afflictions" (2 Cor 1:3–4); "Come to me, all you who labor and are burdened and I will refresh you" (Mt 11:28). These verses are followed by this notation: "The two columns on which I have built my edifice." She found in them what she called the "character" or the "principles of the good God". So she quivered with indignation before formulas that were ill-considered, one-sided, or insufficiently nuanced, which imputed to Providence and its vengeful or purifying designs all the sufferings under which humanity groans.

When a retreat preacher once affirmed that God is responsible for all our trials and that he positively wills them, since he does not prevent them even though he could, she was disturbed by this summary verdict, which seemed to her to be an insult to divine benevolence. This was the beginning of two years of research, in the course of which she turned the question over and over again under all its aspects. She put her thoughts into writing; she critiqued the texts that did not agree with her interpretation. She defined a few firm points: on the whole, suffering is a result of sin; considered in detail, it is, in general, the fact of secondary causes, events, man, and the fallen angels. What was at issue was the direct intervention of God in this matter. Our Céline intended to reduce it as much as possible, somewhat forgetful of the mystery whose secret will be revealed to us in the hereafter alone. In any case, she did not accept—and who would think to blame her for it—having the Father presented as a veritable executioner, skilled at torturing his friends in order to associate them more closely with his Cross. He pities, he comforts, he helps those who weep. In the same manner, she rejected the venturesome reflections, even when signed by illustrious names, that seemed to confer on suffering a certain priority. "Before all else, there is Charity", she exclaims with Saint Paul.

The following is one of numerous passages in which Sister Geneviève expressed this inner struggle in prose that is at times rather breathless and awkward in style:

> It is because of the hardening of our hearts, because of our sins, that our very good God is seen in the hard necessity of handing us over to punishment. Why would any man alive complain? May each one complain of not loving his God enough. May he complain of his sin, since it is on account of our transgressions, our abominations, and our lack of love that we bear the pain. "However," says Scripture, "the Lord does not always reject us; but when he afflicts us, he has compassion according to his great mercy, for it is out of the kindness of his heart that he humbles and afflicts the children of men." We will not know how much it costs him to allow us to suffer; his paternal heart is crushed by it. It is as if he has to turn his head in order not to see his children victim to suffering; but it is for their good. He then arms himself with courage, knowing full well that later on we will not be able to thank him enough with our poor hearts for such a favor.

Sister Geneviève fiercely held to the side of the sequence that affirms the extreme mercy of a God who cannot rejoice over our tears. Old age made her more aware of the other side, which sets down, not only the price of suffering necessary for the ascent of the soul and the redemption of sinners—she had always been convinced of this—but also the direct action of the Lord in awakening the call to crucified love. On February 10, 1956, she wrote to one of her confidants:

> The other night I understood that it was suffering accepted with love that gave value to my life: physical sufferings like those of martyrdom. Up until now I have suffered in all sorts of ways, in mind and in heart, suffered also from difficult and ponderous work, which Saint Paul enumerates in his list of tribulations. But what crowns life is personal suffering, like that of Job, afflicted in his own body. Saint Paul ended his very tormented life by the martyrdom of blood. Our Lord has said: "Was it not necessary that Christ should suffer and so enter into his glory?" Suffering in itself has no value; one has only to look at the demons and those damned. But accepted with loving abandonment to God, it is a divine seal put upon our life. . . . It seemed to me that I saw it clearly, and I thanked God effusively for allowing me to pass through this crucible.

The final trial—while waiting for the light of glory—urged her still farther in the serene understanding of a problem that had so stubbornly haunted her.

V. The Carmelite

In the face of this soul who boldly scrutinized the abysses that even theologians penetrate only with fear and trembling, certain readers will perhaps think to themselves:

"How far we are from the solitary course by which the ascent of Carmel is carried out!" It is evident that such an effort at investigation corresponds very little to the pure principles of Saint John of the Cross. Sister Geneviève rarely read the author of *The Dark Night*. Nevertheless, as we have said, she was a contemplative in her own way, entirely preoccupied with Christ, looking at him, questioning him; embracing him with something close to the Franciscan style of a Saint Bonaventure. The calm view she had of her nothingness had protected her against the risk of imbalance that is a part of unbounded activity.

All the same, Céline understood and deeply loved her Carmelite vocation. On the occasion of her Golden Jubilee, and in response to certain allegations in the book of Maxentius Van der Meersch on the Saint of Lisieux, she gave a testimony that is a magnificent eulogy of the religious vocation. "Despite the often very sharp trials that have marked my path, I find, in the end, that our Lord has not failed in his promise and that 'in leaving all things', I have found not only 'the hundredfold', but I went farther, to 'the thousandfold', in joy and interior peace." She carefully drew up her assessment of the disadvantages and the advantages of such a life; she enumerated the elements that can disturb or expand the climate of a community. Invoking the example of Mother Agnes of Jesus and of Thérèse, she extolled their profound cheerfulness: "In their greatest difficulties, the peace of heaven inundated their souls and fortified them: true happiness was their lot in life as it is with all fervent souls. And there are a great many of them in our cloisters."

On November 30, 1947, she again took up the subject in long manuscript instructions relating to topics for preaching. She wanted something to be said about the beauty of the Carmelite life and the practical virtues it demands, as well as the sublimity and the submissiveness inherent in such close cohabitation, which must become a communion with Christ.

She insisted, in getting down to concrete applications, on the importance of the promises made. "If one examines herself with respect to the vows, she will find that poverty is followed least. 'Everybody's business is nobody's business', said Father Pichon; and it is true because the community belongs to all, without being anyone's in particular." For her part, she erred rather through excessive "conservatism". Skilled as she was, and putting everything to good use, she was not resigned either to destroy things or to see them being destroyed and so set up reserves that she could draw upon at opportune times. "I know", she wrote, "that I am very much a collector. I know immediately what purpose things can serve, even those that don't look like much and that others would throw away. I put them aside in case of need. But it seems to me that I act in this way out of a spirit of order and not because I am attached. It is rather a suffering for me, and I would give my possessions to someone else with great joy." Over and above her Norman background, there was certainly a view of Providence in this matter. How many photographs, documents, and different kinds of objects relating to Thérèse would have been sacrificed as having no value without the saving instinct that animated Céline!

Age would mortify this natural tendency. She who reigned as mistress over the collection of Thérèsian documents and souvenirs, to the point of saying humorously that "the sun did not set on her inventories", was constrained to record the division of her duties.

Having lived for such a long time, my strength was lacking, and my "possessions" were dispersed to this one and that one. Since I am an "archivist" and everyone isn't, it happens, as Scripture says: "that the father accumulates and the son squanders". I have seen that with my own eyes, and I have blessed the good God for having seen it, because if these distributions had taken place after my death, I would not have noticed it, whereas I have felt the detachments one by one. Oh! what a grace!

"To grow old," she wrote, "to have times of being robbed against our will or something borrowed without security but with our consent, to have the time to pick our little pearls along life's way, that has given me consoling thoughts on renunciation, which, contradictory as it may seem, becomes something of incomparable value."

Céline was always careful about asking for permissions and giving an account of things. Authority, for her, had a sacred character. She had respected and loved it under the hand of Mother Marie de Gonzague, who, moreover, had shown a genuine kindness to her. She even watched over her attitude toward the young religious promoted to prioress or sub-prioress. As for Mother Agnes of Jesus, the sisterly affection that she devoted to her never did injury to either the deference or the spirit of obedience due to the superior. Sister Geneviève questioned at times, but she always gave in. Let us say, in the beautiful expression of the moralist Mersch, that, in the realm of her competence, she did not necessarily surrender "the next to the last word" to those in charge— she explained, she argued, she objected; but, always and good-naturedly, she left "the last word" to them.

There was the same docility with regard to the Rule. The Carmelite life has austerities that, in everything, take the form of a network of customs and observances that are often crucifying. Sister Geneviève, as we have seen, had the strength to adapt herself to it. In her old age, she suffered from seeing it infringed upon however slightly.

Above all, she loved the beautiful apostolic inspiration that moved Saint Teresa of Avila in her Reform and that supports the retirement and immolation of the cloister. She spoke of the salvation of souls with such conviction that the Bishop of Saigon, in order to be able to talk with her, wanted to take her to Indochina. The episode of Pranzini[2] had marked her as well as the apostasy of the infamous Father Hyacinthe Loyson, for whom Thérèse had solicited her prayers. After the death of the Saint, she sent this unfortunate ex-priest *The Story of a Soul* and the passages from letters in which her sister mentioned him. She wrote to him twice. He responded, without giving the least room for hope, by sending biographical details and portraits of his pseudohousehold. His death, apparently unrepentant, grieved our Carmelite. She rejoiced, toward the end of her life, in learning certain details that supported the hypothesis of his deathbed conversion.

On October 30, 1909, informed by Dr. La Néele of a grave clerical scandal in the vicinity of Lisieux, Sister Geneviève wrote to Léonie: "It seems to me that it is not the time to abandon a soul when everyone else is abandoning him. How I would wish to be a prison chaplain, in order to go as I pleased to lift up fallen souls! . . . I have much more compassion than distaste for withered lilies. Oh! what we ourselves would be if the good God had not preserved us, for we are capable of anything, absolutely anything!"

Like her Mother, Teresa of Avila, like her parents and her glorious sister, Céline had a Catholic soul. She vibrated with emotion at anything that touched on the kingdom of God. She was a "daughter of the Church", she espoused her cause and all her interests. She professed never to have wanted anything but the truth and requested repeatedly that her writings be burned, "without mercy and with her thanks", if any error

[2] Henri Pranzini was a criminal executed in 1887. Thérèse and her sisters had prayed for his conversion.

were found in them. This apostolic sense, this fidelity to Rome, put the final touch to her interior life. The child that she became in the school of Thérèse would protect to the end this warrior soul, this knight at heart.

8

Come, Lord Jesus

I. Waiting for Death

On July 24, 1897, Sister Geneviève of the Holy Face, alone at the bedside of Thérèse, who was fast approaching death, gave her this confidence: "You are my ideal, and this ideal, I cannot attain. Oh! how sad it is! I am like a little child who is not conscious of distances: in the arms of his mother, he extends his little hand in order to grab hold of a curtain, or some object . . . he has no idea how far away it is!"

"Yes," answered the Saint mysteriously, "but, on the last day, the good God will draw near to his Céline with all that she would have desired, and she will grab hold of everything."

It was, with a different image, the theme of the divine "lift": grace crowning with beauty the persistence of an entire life spent in thankless effort. Céline was going to know this dénouement to the full. For a long time, she had had a presentiment of it, she aspired to it. On December 24, 1926, she wrote to Léonie:

During my thanksgiving, I thought of death, as I usually do, and I said to myself that it was the greatest and most meritorious action of my life, an action I would perform only once. Then, I experienced an immense desire to accomplish this action as perfectly as possible, and I told myself that it would not be enough to die of love in an act of perfect love, but that I wanted it to be such a love that it breaks my bonds.

I then felt certain that I would be heard. God cannot give such desires if he does not want to fulfill them. Truly, I feel totally unworthy of that grace, and my miserable life, which has been wholly external, entirely made up of earthy encumbrances, does not seem to dispose me for it, but it is precisely because of my poverty that this grace seems easier for me to obtain. I will present myself before God, not with empty hands, but with the paraphernalia of all my misdeeds. I am summoning all of my imperfections to my judgment. It is no longer necessary to speak of good actions. I have given them to God as I went along, and he has distributed them to souls. . . . So I will arrive in the procession of all my wretchedness, and God will be so sweet to me that, not being able to stand the sight of such goodness, the bond that was still holding me here on earth will be broken.

The call from on high appeared to sound the next day, on December 12, 1958, where we left Sister Geneviève exhausted by the work to which she had devoted herself in wrapping under seal what was left of the ashes and objects found in the coffin of her parents and which had not been placed in the new tomb. Obviously, she had exceeded her strength. Her spirit alone sustained her. "I truly do not know what's wrong with me today", she sighed. Before the day ended, she wanted, at length and with exquisite tenderness, to thank the sister who for so many years had been her devoted infirmarian. She added gravely: "I have finished all that I had to do; now, the good God can take me."

After a restless night, she awoke in a state of extreme weakness, her pulse no more than twenty-five. The doctor was called immediately and pronounced the case to be very serious, even hopeless. She could not contain her joy. "Today is *Gaudete* Sunday. Rejoice, the Lord is near. Yes, yes, he is coming for me. Oh! what happiness! I have been waiting for him for such a long time!"

One felt vibrating in her the dream of eternity that had always possessed her. "I want to see God", Teresa of Avila had cried when, as a little girl, she was overtaken on the road to the Moors, leaving with her young brother in search of martyrdom. "I want to see God", sang the soul of Céline, faced with her great day of reckoning.

Because the shrine chapel was being repaired, the statue of the Virgin of the Smile had been brought down and taken into the infirmary, which made our invalid feel that she was receiving a visit from Mary. In the evening, Sister Geneviève received extreme unction, following attentively the rites and the prayers of the priest. On December 14, the new clocks at the Abbey of the Benedictines in Lisieux were blessed. Céline had sponsored one of them. Had her "godchild" sounded her departure for heaven?

Powerful remedies mastered the crisis for the time being, but the causes of her illness remained: myocardial insufficiency and arrhythmia complicated by renal deficiency and congestion of the lungs. The diagnosis remained most pessimistic: the least mishap could, in a flash, carry the patient off. She was watched over continuously, sitting during the day in her armchair and, in the night, in her bed, which she did not leave during the last five weeks of her life.

It was said that her illness disconcerted all expectations. Since she was an elderly person close to ninety years old and tired out from infirmities and work, an imminent and peaceful end might have been expected, like a candle being extinguished. But Sister Geneviève lived on for seventy-five more days of this struggle against death, and she would endure true torments of both body and soul with perfect lucidity.

From the moment she was incapacitated and condemned

to an immobility particularly painful for such an active person, she showed an inalterable sweetness in bravely bearing her multiple sufferings; she also manifested total availability in regard to all who came near her. She acquiesced to every treatment, was careful to give the least possible trouble to those around her, overcame lassitude or distress, embellishing her remarks with infectious good humor, and was troubled only by the fatigue of those who did not spare themselves at her bedside. Opinions were unanimous in this respect. Here is one particularly authoritative assessment, dated December 25:

> Happy, lucid, courageous, interested in everything, eager for details and explanations . . . about everything just as much as about heaven, her beautiful smile, her patience in suffering show to what point authentic spiritual childhood inspires her. She has a radiance of youth about her that does good to those who approach her. Truly, after having given witness by her writings and her depositions, she witnesses by her own life at a time when one does not put on an act. Everything about her, moreover, is simple and spontaneous.

In order to be complete, it is necessary to add that the religious appointed to care for Sister Geneviève spared neither time nor trouble and demonstrated admirable devotion and tenderness, profiting in addition from the lessons of such a death. As for the community, they courageously faced the extra work that the situation necessitated. Around her deathbed, there was moral unanimity and an impulse of charity, of which all cherished the memory.

II. The Unspeakable Trial

There were three phases in her long agony: up until January 18, there were alternating periods of alertness and remission—from this date until February 5, there were crises of suffering in a mysterious interior trial—then a relative easing that ended abruptly with death.

During the first weeks, unable to feed herself, sustained by injections, shaken by uncontrollable vomiting that tired her excessively, Sister Geneviève waited with cheerful serenity for the moment of the great encounter. "If I fall into a coma," she said on December 23, "my death will not be very beautiful perhaps, but I think that it is now what counts, and I see clearly that God is helping me; I feel calm and full of confidence." When the Mother Prioress declared that the fruits of spiritual childhood were evident in her, she humbly remarked:

> Perhaps Little Thérèse wants to show in her Céline that one can remain little and simple even in extreme old age. But one must always say: "It is you, Lord, who have accomplished all our works." Yes, it is he alone, for I could well be caught up in the temptation to sadness as well as to fear. It is true that I have no fear at all, none at all, of God. Oh! I am going to be so happy to see him, to see his Humanity! I have desired him so much! Yet, I have much offended him; but, even so, I'm not afraid, and I summon all of my wretchedness to his Tribunal. I am very sure that Jesus will say to me as to the woman in the Gospel: Go, my daughter, your sins are forgiven!

The same evening, she returned to this subject: "Yes, I believe that God wants to show how pleased he is with those who walk in the 'little way' of humility, simplicity, and confidence, and so he helps them in time of trial, for, of ourselves, we are good for nothing."

"I see as clear as day", she continued saying, "that only spiritual childhood can give us true peace of heart and the grace to be like a little child in the hands of God."

On Christmas eve, the thoughts of Mercy took hold of her. "How can you want me to be afraid of God? I have always centered my life on him. I recall that when someone brought me the picture of the Holy Shroud of Turin, I wept with joy at seeing his true face. I have tried to paint it; but now I will really and truly see it. I believe that I will 'die again' of happiness. And also to see the truth of all things; I, who have always hungered and thirsted for justice."

For a long time, she meditated on the beautiful prophetic verses: "His rising is certain as the dawn" (Hosea). "Yes, on you, Yahweh will rise, and his glory will shine on you; your Sun will no longer set, but Yahweh will be for you an eternal light, and your God will be your glory. I, Yahweh, I will hasten these things in their day" (Isaiah).

"I cannot tell you", she wrote, "how my heart beats at these words; they surpass every sentiment. . . . May it be my God who is my glory." Up until the end, she was encouraged by these phrases of hope. On Christmas Day, everything had a sweet air about it. "I am like a weary traveler", she said, "who finally sees the doors to her father's house open before her."

On the feast of Saint Stephen, a religious showed her a picture of her little nephew, a baby of three months sitting on his mother's lap. She was very moved by it and could not take her eyes off it.

That is my image; that is just the way I want to be in the arms of God. That child is there, surrendered, with all his weakness, and it is just because of that that his mother has pity on him and presses him to her heart with so much love. If he were a little bigger, he could fend for himself, and his mother would have less pity for him. It is like this little one that I want to be; and God my Father, my dear Papa, will take me in his arms. I will have his pity. To have his pity is everything.

The doctor, whom she asked if the Lord would come soon to take her, declared that she was "unique", that he had indeed seen sick persons desire death, but only to escape suffering, while she wished for it in order to see God.

Sister Geneviève, who kept under her very resolute character a delightful ingenuousness, had the custom of bringing each year to a close by writing the words: "Joseph, Mary, Jesus", wanting the Divine Name to be her last thought. On January 1, the same formula, but reversed, served as her first greeting to those whom she loved more than anything else. For the last time, she performed this rite, putting into it all her filial piety. She had, on that day, the happy surprise of a telegram from Pope John XXIII, bringing her, "as token of the abundant graces of peace and abandonment to God a special Apostolic Blessing".

On January 18, it was noticed that she kept her left eye closed. They asked her if she had a pain in it. "Why, no," she stated with precision in a detached tone of voice, "it's dead. . . . But that doesn't mean anything. . . . I have given it to God. Oh! there's no need to be cross with it for lying down, because it has really worked during its life; and at present, it couldn't do anything; so I thank God for it."

When it was said to her: "Your whole family is preparing to welcome you", she answered: "Yes, I will be very happy about that, but what interests me the most by far is our Lord and the Blessed Virgin . . . to know everything about her, about her life, I cannot even think of it!" In the evening, in a rather unexpected manner, new and alarming symptoms manifested themselves. She welcomed this sudden worsening with her most beautiful smile.

The next day, at her request, her infirmarian asked the gardener to pardon her for all the trouble that she had given him when she was busy with her work. She still received the community with a mixture of affection and cheerfulness, which accentuated her astonishing presence of mind. Thinking about Saint Sebastian, whose feast was approaching, she intoned the old refrain:

O great Saint Sebastian
To whom God refuses nothing . . .

Would he not usher her into the hereafter? It was a vain hope. Such a prospect for Sister Geneviève was thwarted for the moment. Keenly disappointed, she exclaimed: "I am going to do as Saint Sebastian; I am going to be healed of my first wounds. I will die not believing in my death."

On the twenty-first, in a conversation with the Mother Prioress, she persisted in stressing the main role of humility in spiritual childhood. She added: "Humility has been the companion of my life; it is by humility that I have entered into the little way. Humility is the carpet on which I have always wished to walk."

The next day, she was able to receive the Sacred Host in the afternoon. But the most painful period of her illness was beginning. That state, approaching the agony, lasted more than fifteen days. Increasingly weakened, tortured by thirst and no longer able to drink, racked by interior burning and undergoing the sharp needles of rheumatism, Sister Geneviève also experienced in her very depths a sense of being utterly forsaken. "When will the door open for me? Does God still love me, since he is not coming to take me? Oh! my Thérèse, look at my distress!" She felt a violent pounding in her back. "How can you not hear?" she groaned. She begged, repeatedly, for someone to light the blessed candle and to throw holy water on her.

It became impossible for her to receive communion daily. She herself had taken down from the wall her small crucifix, which she kept from this time on in her right hand, without ever relaxing her hold on it during the course of those weeks of dreadful interior crisis. From time to time, she brought it to her lips, murmuring in a broken voice, syllable by syllable, in order to encourage herself: "Break the web of this sweet encounter. O my Jesus, I want to love you with all my heart, unto folly, with all my strength; yes, with all my strength, unto folly. . . ." In the same manner, she clung to the rosary entwined around her fingers and gripped it with all her faith.

She offered this martyrdom for her parents' Cause. "It is not to see them exalted. Oh, no! It is to do some good for Christian families. I have always sought only the glory of God; yes, to make him known and loved." She also prayed for priests, who had always been one of her principal concerns. It was suggested that she think about Christian unity and the Ecumenical Council that the Pope had just publicly announced his intention of convoking. She appeared very interested and gasped in one breath: "One flock, one shepherd!"

The mystery of suffering revealed to her all its secrets now that she was totally plunged into the furnace. Her countenance was transformed. She assumed expressions that struck the religious who came to see her at intervals. Her thoughts showed that her soul was, in every sense, going right in the direction of Calvary: "How much it costs! I had so much desired martyrdom, wanted the Passion."

"It is God who does it."

"He is good, the good God! Oh! He is good!"

The question that had always troubled her, that of the direct intervention of heaven in our human sufferings, found its solution, when she looked at it from the perspective of one who is dying, in a sort of higher intuition, in a personal experience that, uniting everything all together to Christ and his Cross, showed her that Love sacrifices through love. She herself stressed it in recalling the notes in which she had recorded her thoughts on this matter. "It is only love united to suffering that counts. Yes, love united to suffering." "It is Jesus who wills it." "*Amor Sacerdos immolat* (Love is the Priest who sacrifices)." This verse of the Paschal hymn consoled her.

Until February 5, Sister Geneviève was in the winepress awaiting a death forever postponed. Her heart failed, then started up again, making her feel that she was suffocating. She had, she said, "a chest full of water". The swelling of her body, the rheumatic pains in one leg and in her heels, made it unbearable for her to stay in bed; her weakness prevented her from leaving it. To all that was added anxiety of soul subject to a strange working that wrested plaintive cries from her: "It is indefinable, inexpressible! . . . How difficult it is! . . . how long it is! . . . how cruel it is! . . ." Then, all of a sudden: "Jesus, I have been in love with him. I want to love him passionately." Then, as they moistened her mouth with ice: "I am thirsting for the waters of eternal life", she sighed, as though speaking to herself.

When she was praised for her courage and when reference was made to her dying of love, she rectified it on the spot, quoting a text from the prophet Isaiah: "In all our works, Lord, it is you who have accomplished them for us." On January 27, she was heard to murmur: "A little lamb on the funeral pyre! Oh! have pity, my Jesus! I feel changes in me that are not natural and that cannot be explained. It is like a breath of fire and a breath of ice." "And don't you feel that God is helping you?" they gently prodded on their part. "Oh! no! not at all. I have only you, my dear sisters, who are comforting me. Otherwise, all is hidden." She was concerned about those who were caring for her, their fatigue, their meals, their rest: "They will not hold up!"

Outside of certain moments of prostration, she did not lose her lively spirit. She still had incisive words, remarks full of originality, which made the doctors smile as much as they surprised and edified them: "It is written in the Gospel that our Lord inclined his head and died. So do I; I try to incline my head, but alas! death does not come." When they took her pulse, she asked: "How's my old heart getting on?" When asking what she called her "staff" for a little water, she sang the popular refrain: "Friends are not so crazy that they go away without having a drink!" "Never", one person observed, "have I seen anyone dying be so amusing." "Nor so full of suffering", she hastened to add.

At certain times, the pains that rarely left her became intense. Overwhelmed but not discouraged, she turned to heaven: "What anguish! My God, my God, why have you abandoned me? I am not dying in ecstasy. I am suffering distress . . . of body and soul. My God! Have pity on me." Then again: "I feel symptoms of death and attacks of life."

The people around her came to hope for the inevitable outcome. She herself begged that nothing be done to prolong her life. "I cannot be better prepared, and all is so much at peace!" Her confidence remained unshaken. "O my God, you know my folly, and my faults are not hidden from you, but you will forgive me everything . . . everything . . . everything. . . ."

On January 30, she thought she was dying; but once more, life did not want to leave her. "I have shivers all over, some are scalding like fire and others are freezing. I am on a red-hot grill like Saint Lawrence. My legs seem dead . . . my blood is no longer circulating. I am going through a real martyrdom." Then, looking tenderly at those who were caring for her she said: "And you are going through it with me! . . . My God, have pity on my little infirmarians!" "This is an agony to be reckoned with", she sighed on February 3. "But I would not want to suffer less. . . ." Several times she repeated: "When am I going to give up my soul? . . . It is a scourge."

The desire to see Jesus increased in her, in the manner of an all-consuming flame. Was it the last purification, like an image of purgatory? Or rather the consummation of a vehement desire to redeem sinners and to cooperate in the mission of Thérèse? In this unusual resistance of the organism to all the forces of destruction, in this fervent charity that neither disappointments nor the night of faith could impair, those who witnessed it sensed obscurely that there was some powerful supernatural force at work. A note dated February 3 conveyed this unanimous impression. It came from the Mother Prioress of the Carmel:

As Sister Geneviève said to me: "How low I am!" I answered: "Reduced to nothing and in extreme humiliation." "Oh! yes, that's it exactly—but Saint John of the Cross says very precisely that that's when the soul attains the highest state possible in this life.—Yes, but I don't feel it!"

The letter continues:

What an identification with Jesus on Calvary! It is the most profoundly moving and enlightening thing that I have ever experienced in religious life. What glory awaits her!

III. *The Victim of Love*

February 5 marked the sixty-fourth anniversary of Sister Geneviève's clothing with the religious habit. The vomiting had ceased momentarily, and she was able to receive Holy Communion. She welcomed the community graciously when they came to greet her on her "funeral pyre". Her eyelids heavy with fatigue, she apologized amusingly, reciting two lines of a verse that she herself and Thérèse had once put up in Léonie's room when they were very tired:

> My eyes are closed to the light of day
> When, after my dinner, I stroll not away.

Although both lungs were congested and her heart was extremely weak and irregular, it seemed that the case was in a slight remission. The noose had been loosened a little bit. The sisters spoke to her about the telegrams they had received from anxious friends, about the requests for news coming from all sides. She had a mischievous smile. "That tells you how my death will be greeted with acts of thanksgiving! But it is once again I who will greet it with the least noise." As they speculated about the future:

"Oh! let's not talk about that", she protested; "so many dates have been advanced, and they came to nothing. . . . It's much ado about nothing." She thought with melancholy about missed opportunity: "Oh! how is it that in such a precarious life and at ninety years of age, a person cannot let go?"

On February 10, finding that she was a little less tired, she called to mind the tragic days that she had lived through: "I still suffer, but it is not the same. You cannot know. I think the devil was given a certain permission to torment me. I can't understand why you did not hear the dull but very hard knocks he gave me. . . . Fortunately, he can do nothing at all because the Lord is fighting for me." On the eleventh, she made this humble and resigned reflection: "When will God, in his great goodness, decide that I have suffered enough?"

On February 13, the Mother Prioress read her a letter from a religious who, in danger of losing her vocation, rejoiced to learn that the sister of Saint Thérèse was thinking about her. "Does she scorn me?" she asked. The invalid raised her arms and repeated several times: "Scorn her! Why, I love her; yes, I love her, and I will always pray for her; tell her that."

The change for the better that began on February 5 became more pronounced each day. The congestion of the lungs had practically disappeared, as well as the uremia. Her features were no longer drawn. The invalid had recovered her normal voice. Although she was able to take only a little liquid, her strength seemed to return. However, she continued to have all kinds of difficulties, particularly sharp rheumatic pains in her feet. She still knew hours of cruel suffering. "Oh! tell me," she asked on February 17, "is it today that my Sun will no longer set? . . . O happy morning when it will be said: Sister Geneviève is dead!"

The next day, since she expressed the desire insistently, the doctor tried to seat her in her armchair. She made a valiant effort but had to admit that her legs could hardly support her. When she had reached her bed again, she judged herself fortunate, like Saint Thomas, for having experienced herself what she was capable of. This same day, she said in a playful tone of voice: "Since they don't want me up there, well! I'm going to eat!" And she proceeded to give a detailed menu, being careful to add: "while waiting until God, in his great goodness, finds that he has time to come for me." This was the final expression of abandonment. After so many feverish desires, she arrived at holy indifference, which was left totally to the divine will. Undoubtedly, this Master was only waiting for the supreme testimony of love before coming to take her.

Now, more than ever, she offered no resistance, accepting the constraints and the distressing rhythm of the life of an invalid. As they propped her up in bed with pillows, she exclaimed: "Do I ever feel imprisoned! . . . with four, five, and six exclamation points! . . . Still, I must be reasonable." And on the same day: "After all, what would it do me to leave here? This is where the good God wants me."

On the twenty-second, she confided to her faithful infirmarian:

> I am only thinking of all that has happened to me in this illness. I assure you it has been very mysterious. You remember when you said to me: "My little Céline, perhaps God will come for you this evening!" While listening to you, I said to myself: "Now, let me see; am I Céline? Did I exist? Did I have a personality?" If you knew how locked away I had been, far from everything! You could never have any idea of it. Oh! how strange it was! and what suffering! One cannot imagine it. It makes me think of a story that Thérèse and I used to read when we were little girls.

And she started to repeat this account, but her energy quickly fell off. On the twenty-third, the community was struck by the exhaustion that marked her face. The twenty-fourth was the anniversary of her profession, and the chaplain brought her Holy Communion. Since he had extended his anniversary greetings to her in a letter, she thanked him with a smile. She continuously admired two beautiful bouquets of flowers providentially offered at the turn the day before. On the same morning, she suffered an attack of suffocation accompanied by a most alarming drop in blood pressure. The doctor judged her to be in imminent danger. Despite her weakness and her total exhaustion, the dying nun remained completely lucid. In the afternoon, she had the sister who was caring for her come close to her so she could tell her: "I believe, all the same, that this time it's for good. Oh! what happiness!" As they were preparing to give her an injection, she remarked sweetly: "Why don't you let the lamp go out little by little since I am not suffering, and all is peaceful?"

Watched continually by her sisters in prayer, she passed the night peacefully, happy at the promise of deliverance. At dawn, she was a little restless but was not suffering. "It is surely today", the Mother Prioress said to her. "Today!" she repeated as though savoring her joy. "Yes, you are struggling; it is a hard fight! But you will have the victory because Jesus is with you." With a triumphal tone and a clouded gaze, but extremely lucid, Sister Geneviève repeated: "Jesus!" This was her last word. It expressed the tenderness of her whole life.

A light sweat formed beads of perspiration on her forehead. Her face, nevertheless, was peaceful, almost radiant. Toward nine o'clock, the community recited the Act of Oblation to Merciful Love. The invalid indicated by signs that she was uniting herself to it. When the doctor arrived, the community of sisters left. It was then that, suddenly very still, propped up against her pillows, Sister Geneviève opened wide her luminous eyes and looked upward with sweet elation. This made such an impression on the doctor that he knelt down, then withdrew, understanding that it was the end. The community immediately returned and were able to contemplate this scene, which lasted from eight to ten minutes. There was a sort of majesty in this dying nun, a sovereign tranquility in which one could see the cer-

"Your sun shall no longer set, for Yahweh will be for you an everlasting light, and your God will be your glory!" — a text from Isaiah that Sister Geneviève held particularly dear

tainty of the tender welcome that the Father would give her. Her bearing remained resolute, her head upright, until her death. Only her breathing, which faded imperceptibly away, and a slight contraction of her throat marked her departure. It was Wednesday, February 25, 1959, at 9:25 A.M. Sister Geneviève of the Holy Face was eighty-nine years and ten months old.

IV. The Funeral Ceremonies

No sooner had she died than the tolling of the bells of the basilica echoed those of the Carmel, but there was something triumphal in the midst of this sorrow. The radio announced the news and, from all sides, telegrams of condolence poured in. That of Pope John XXIII, who had formerly presided at the jubilee of the dead sister, was especially marked with touching and paternal tenderness.

The body was on view in the interior choir, where the nuns said their Office, until the evening of the twenty-seventh. During the three days, there was a constant stream of people. Some came from quite a distance, even from other countries. They did not tire of contemplating, behind the grille, that face that Thérèse had loved so much and that bore, along with the imprint of the cross, a majestic serenity. "That is as good as a retreat for us", observed some of those present.

The funeral ceremonies were set for Saturday, February 28. Four bishops were in attendance: they were from Bayeux and Evreux, the Auxiliary of Sées, and Bishop Fallaize. After the Mass, His Excellency, Bishop Jacquemin, Ordinary of the place, mounted the pulpit in order to emphasize the exceptional bonds of intimacy that had united Sister Geneviève to her glorious little sister. He stressed above all the final lesson of this life and this death: the sovereign efficacy of the way of spiritual childhood in order to bring the soul to the summits of divine union and to make her apostolate fruitful.

The numerous clergy then moved into the cloister and lined up in the choir in front of the religious. The three absolutions were sung without accompaniment by the Carmelite Fathers. The first was given by the Very Reverend Father Paul Philippe, Commissary General of the Holy Office, who was, at the time, the representative of the Holy See and the personal delegate of His Eminence Cardinal Ottaviani; the second was given by the Very Reverend Father General of the Discalced Carmelites; and the third by His Excellency, Bishop Jacquemin.

The Carmelite Fathers, clothed in their white mantles, then took up the coffin and carried it to the entrance of the vault, under the shrine chapel, where Mother Agnes of Jesus and Sister Marie of the Sacred Heart already reposed in the shadow of Thérèse. A verse from one of the psalms engraved in stone guards their final sleep. Sister Geneviève herself had chosen it because it expressed her eternal dream, at last realized: "You have hidden us, Lord, in the secret of your Face."

INDEX

Page numbers in *italics* refer to illustrations.